Katherine M. Shelfer
Editor

Business Reference Services and Sources: How End Users and Librarians Work Together

Pre-Publication REVIEWS, COMMENTARIES, EVALUATIONS . . .

Business Reference Services and Sources: How End Users and Librarians Work Together

Forthcoming topics in *The Reference Librarian* series:

• Philosophies of Reference Service, Number 59

Published:

Business Reference Services and Sources: How End Users and Librarians Work Together

Katherine M. Shelfer
Editor

The Haworth Press, Inc.
New York • London

Business Reference Services and Sources: How End Users and Librarians Work Together has also been published as *The Reference Librarian*, Number 58 1997.

The development, preparation, and publication of this work has been undertaken with great care. However, the publisher, employees, editors, and agents of The Haworth Press and all imprints of The Haworth Press, Inc., including The Haworth Medical Press and The Pharmaceutical Products Press, are not responsible for any errors contained herein or for consequences that may ensue from use of materials or information contained in this work. Opinions expressed by the author(s) are not necessarily those of The Haworth Press, Inc.

Cover design by Thomas J. Mayshock Jr.

The Haworth Press, Inc., 10 Alice Street, Binghamton, NY 13904-1580 USA

Library of Congress Cataloging-in-Publication Data

Business reference services and sources: how end users and librarians work together/Katherine M. Shelfer, editor.
    p. cm.
    Also published as The reference librarian, no. 58, 1997.
    Includes bibliographical references and index.
    ISBN 0-7890-0359-7
    1. Business–Information services. 2. Business–Bibliography–Methodology. 3. Reference services (Libraries) 4. Reference books–Business. 5. Business libraries. I. Shelfer, Katherine M. II. Reference librarian.
Z675.B8B88 1997
027.6'9--dc21
                                                      97-29668
                                                           CIP

INDEXING & ABSTRACTING

Contributions to this publication are selectively indexed or abstracted in print, electronic, online, or CD-ROM version(s) of the reference tools and information services listed below. This list is current as of the copyright date of this publication. See the end of this section for additional notes.

- *Academic Abstracts/CD-ROM,* EBSCO Publishing Editorial Department, P.O. Box 590, Ipswich, MA 01938-0590

- *Academic Search: data base of 2,000 selected academic serials, updated monthly:* EBSCO Publishing, 83 Pine Street, Peabody, MA 01960

- *CNPIEC Reference Guide: Chinese National Directory of Foreign Periodicals,* P.O. Box 88, Beijing, People's Republic of China

- *Current Awareness Abstracts,* Association for Information Management, Information House, 20-24 Old Street, London EC1V 9AP, England

- *Current Index to Journals in Education,* Syracuse University, 4-194 Center for Science and Technology, Syracuse, NY 13244-4100

- *Educational Administration Abstracts (EAA),* Sage Publications, Inc., 2455 Teller Road, Newbury Park, CA 91320

- *IBZ International Bibliography of Periodical Literature,* Zeller Verlag GmbH & Co., P.O.B. 1949, d-49009 Osnabruck, Germany

- *Index to Periodical Articles Related to Law,* University of Texas, 727 East 26th Street, Austin, TX 78705

- *Information Science Abstracts,* Plenum Publishing Company, 233 Spring Street, New York, NY 10013-1578

- *Informed Librarian, The,* Infosources Publishing, 140 Norma Road, Teaneck, NJ 07666

- *INSPEC Information Services,* Institution of Electrical Engineers, Michael Faraday House, Six Hills Way, Stevenage, Herts SG1 2AY, England

(continued)

- *INTERNET ACCESS (& additional networks) Bulletin Board for Libraries ("BUBL") coverage of information resources on INTERNET, JANET, and other networks.*
  - <URL:http://bubl.ac.uk/>
  - The new locations will be found under <URL:http://bubl.ac.uk/link/>.
  - Any existing BUBL users who have problems finding information on the new service should contact the BUBL help line by sending e-mail to <bubl@bubl.ac.uk>.
  The Andersonian Library, Curran Building, 101 St. James Road, Glasgow G4 0NS, Scotland

- *Journal of Academic Librarianship: Guide to Professional Literature, The,* Grad School of Library & Information Science/Simmons College, 300 The Fenway, Boston, MA 02115-5898

- *Konyvtari Figyelo-Library Review,* National Szechenyi Library, Centre for Library and Information Science, H-1827 Budapest, Hungary

- *Library & Information Science Abstracts (LISA),* Bowker-Saur Limited, Maypole House, Maypole Road, East Grinstead, West Sussex, RH19 1HH England

- *Library Literature,* The H.W. Wilson Company, 950 University Avenue, Bronx, NY 10452

- *MasterFILE: updated database from EBSCO Publishing,* EBSCO Publishing, 83 Pine Street, Peabody, MA 01960

- *Newsletter of Library and Information Services,* China Sci-Tech Book Review, Library of Academia Sinica, 8 Kexueyuan Nanlu, Zhongguancun, Beijing 100080, People's Republic of China

- *OT BibSys,* American Occupational Therapy Foundation, P.O. Box 31220, Bethesda, MD 20824-1220

- *Referativnyi Zhurnal (Abstracts Journal of the Institute of Scientific Information of the Republic of Russia),* The Institute of Scientific Information, Baltijskaja ul., 14, Moscow A-219, Republic of Russia

- *Sage Public Administration Abstracts (SPAA),* Sage Publications, Inc., 2455 Teller Road, Newbury Park, CA 91320

(continued)

SPECIAL BIBLIOGRAPHIC NOTES

related to special journal issues (separates)
and indexing/abstracting

- ☐ indexing/abstracting services in this list will also cover material in any "separate" that is co-published simultaneously with Haworth's special thematic journal issue or DocuSerial. Indexing/abstracting usually covers material at the article/chapter level.

- ☐ monographic co-editions are intended for either non-subscribers or libraries which intend to purchase a second copy for their circulating collections.

- ☐ monographic co-editions are reported to all jobbers/wholesalers/approval plans. The source journal is listed as the "series" to assist the prevention of duplicate purchasing in the same manner utilized for books-in-series.

- ☐ to facilitate user/access services all indexing/abstracting services are encouraged to utilize the co-indexing entry note indicated at the bottom of the first page of each article/chapter/contribution.

- ☐ this is intended to assist a library user of any reference tool (whether print, electronic, online, or CD-ROM) to locate the monographic version if the library has purchased this version but not a subscription to the source journal.

- ☐ individual articles/chapters in any Haworth publication are also available through the Haworth Document Delivery Services (HDDS).

Business Reference Services and Sources: How End Users and Librarians Work Together

CONTENTS

ABOUT THE EDITOR

Katherine M. Shelfer is University Librarian for Business and Economics in the Strozier Library at the Florida State University in Tallahassee, Florida. She has written and been published extensively in the area of information and business-related matters.

Introduction

Katherine M. Shelfer

We don't need a supercomputer to calculate that libraries and reference services are undergoing seismic upheaval as information access changes. Susan Bjorner (1996) wrote,

> For years we've been struggling to push the walls of the library down and open it up to more use . . . aided by technology we're succeeding. . . . Users are willing and anxious to become our collaborators—or competitors—in the information arena. . . . we have important and unique skills to bring to the playing field. . . . We just need to apply them in a different, faster-paced, more populated environment. . . .

Today, remote access gives people alternative ways to find information. Nobody has to come to the library. In fact, they are being discouraged from it. Libraries and librarians are again the focus of negative advertising campaigns (Packard, 1997). Vendors give lip service to the value of libraries and librarians, but at they same time, they market their wares directly to the public as a means of avoiding both. Some library schools are even taking "library" out of their names!

In such a climate, reference librarians face a challenge. We need to demonstrate that we are not as useless to research as buggy whips are to jets. To do that, we need to be proactive. We need to sell researchers on the value-added that we bring to the research process. We need to convey the message that the reference librarian-customer relationship is synergistic.

I believe very strongly that the reference librarian's role should be that

---

[Haworth co-indexing entry note]: "Introduction." Shelfer, Katherine M. Co-published simultaneously in *The Reference Librarian* (The Haworth Press, Inc.) No. 58, 1997, pp. 1-3; and: *Business Reference Services and Sources: How End Users and Librarians Work Together* (ed: Katherine M. Shelfer) The Haworth Press, Inc., 1997, pp. 1-3. Single or multiple copies of this article are available for a fee from The Haworth Document Delivery Service [1-800-342-9678, 9:00 a.m. - 5:00 p.m. (EST). E-mail address: getinfo@haworth.com].

of a team player in the research process. The healthiest partnership is not a one-night stand, it is ongoing. But how do librarians and users work together? How are such partnerships built?

We must begin seeing end-users as people, not as desk statistics. As Crawford and Barrett write, "Strategic alliances are proliferating in the corporate world. They offer the participants an opportunity to pool limited resources, skills and capabilities to achieve common objectives that the partners may well be unable to achieve working alone" (p. 75). Reference librarians have always been able to point to specific and concrete examples of times when their assistance made a positive contribution to the needs of others. We just need to be more vocal about it. We need to market ourselves.

Our marketing efforts must reach our end-users at the point of their need. A student assistant once told me that reference librarians belong on the desk and students belong in the back room doing the support functions. He couldn't understand why it was reversed. I will take it one step more. Why are we in the building all the time? After all, the front lines for reference service have clearly moved beyond it!

The good news is that many reference librarians have been proactive in the development of resources to assist remote users. They have been willing to "grow feet" and leave the comfort of their reference desk to enter classrooms and join manufacturing teams. They have reached across the country to provide resources. They have reached beyond the accepted and acceptable primary user population to embrace "outsiders." And they have been rewarded!

This volume demonstrates through co-authored papers and reports of collaborative projects between librarians and end-users, that the strategic alliance concept is alive and well. Three articles address the development and use of Internet sites. Welch and King report on a project in which librarians and a management professor combined forces. The librarians developed an Internet resource site and provided instruction in U.S. business research to non-native speakers. They used citation analysis to evaluate the results. The students produced high-quality papers and held stimulating and challenging discussions in the classroom which improved their communication skills.

Shelfer and Crawford report on their project to create a web site for school business officials. In this case the academic business reference librarian elected to provide extended service to an unaffiliated patron. This service resulted in direct benefits to the librarian's primary user population. LaRose reports on the benefits of using corporate web pages to supplement traditional business resources when working with users.

In their paper, Medaris and Manley view networking in the people sense. They describe a collaboration between a Small Business Development Center (SBDC) and a library in which the librarians assist product developers with patent and trademark searches, technology and other market research. Many clients of this partnership have successfully launched products and services. Bennett and Napp report on three successful projects in which the information specialists were integral members of a customer-librarian partnership at the National Center for Manufacturing Sciences.

Atkinson and Figueroa describe a joint research project in which a librarian and a student collaborated on a study to investigate library use and research behavior of business students. Crawford and Barrett describe a strategic alliance between a librarian and a business professor which works. Huett, Sims and Villalon describe a cooperative venture between librarians, faculty and students to avoid information overload in business research instruction. Simmons and MacDonald describe a partnership between reference librarians, acquisition librarians and faculty which ensure that curricular needs in a small Florida college are satisfied.

This series of papers included faculty, students, external users, non-librarian supervisors, and other librarians as co-authors. Clearly, collaboration is alive and well. I wish there were more of it in the literature to enlighten and inspire.

REFERENCES

Bjorner, Susanne. "Changing Roles? Changing Worlds!" *Online* 20, 5, 8, Sept.-Oct. 1996.
"Packard Bell Pulls Offensive Ad." *Cognotes* Issue IV, Feb. 1997.

BUSINESS SERVICES
AND THE INTERNET

Using the Internet to Teach
U.S. Business Research
to Students of English
as a Second Language

Jeanie M. Welch
William E. King

SUMMARY. The American Graduate School of International Management (Thunderbird) has an extensive English as a second language (ESL) program for graduate students. As a component of the content-based aspect of this program, students have a semester-long project involving finding information about a U.S. company and its

Jeanie M. Welch is Associate Professor and Reference Unit Head, J. Murrey Atkins Library, UNC Charlotte, Charlotte, NC 28223. William E. King is Associate Professor of English, Department of Modern Languages, American Graduate School of International Management, Thunderbird Campus, Glendale, AZ 85306.

[Haworth co-indexing entry note]: "Using the Internet to Teach U.S. Business Research to Students of English as a Second Language." Welch, Jeanie M., and William E. King. Co-published simultaneously in *The Reference Librarian* (The Haworth Press, Inc.) No. 58, 1997, pp. 5-12; and: *Business Reference Services and Sources: How End Users and Librarians Work Together* (ed: Katherine M. Shelfer) The Haworth Press, Inc., 1997, pp. 5-12. Single or multiple copies of this article are available for a fee from The Haworth Document Delivery Service [1-800-342-9678, 9:00 a.m. - 5:00 p.m. (EST). E-mail address: getinfo@haworth.com].

place in its industry. The students must include information about corporate finance, marketing, corporate history, and an industry and competitor analysis. A business librarian at another institution created a website for a course in competitor analysis. A business librarian at another institution created a website for a course with a similar assignment; this website included hot links to sources of U.S. corporate and industrial data. This article discusses the structuring of the course, the creation of the website, the collaboration between the classroom instructor and the business librarian, and the effects of the website on the quality and quantity of the ESL students' research. *[Article copies available for a fee from The Haworth Document Delivery Service: 1-800-342-9678. E-mail address: getinfo@haworth.com]*

This article brings together two new realities of reference service–service to a diverse user population and the integration of new technologies into reference service and library instruction. One of the challenges that reference librarians face is dealing with patrons for whom English is a second language. Another challenge is integrating the possibilities of the Internet into their reference and library instruction functions. Working closely with classroom teachers of English as a second language and integrating a course-specific website into a research project can be beneficial in meeting both of these challenges.

THE CLASSROOM SETTING

Background

Founded in 1946 and located just outside of Phoenix Arizona, the American Graduate School of Informational Management (also known as Thunderbird) is a non-profit, private graduate school dedicated to offering a graduate management program distinguished by its multilingual, cross-cultural, and global business components. It is accredited by both the American Assembly of Collegiate Schools of Business and by the North Central Association of Colleges and Schools. It offers the Master of Informational Management (MIM) as its primary degree and two specialized degrees: the Master of Informational Health Management and the Master of Informational Management of Technology. As of Fall, 1995, there were 1,450 full-time graduate students enrolled in the Thunderbird program, with 30% of those being students from countries other than the United States. Thunderbird has survived on the principle that doing business means the ability to speak a foreign language, with an understanding of the customs and of the intricacies required of international business management. The curricula of the three departments (World Business, International Studies, and Modern Languages) are, therefore, heavily integrated to be responsive to the need of corporate enterprises.

A very important part of the graduate program is the alumni network of chartered alumni groups worldwide. The network, connected through CompuServe, allows students, faculty, alumni and staff to converse on-line about course projects, curriculum development, conferences, and reunions. This network serves as the "centerpiece" for interactive programs to bring alumni on-line in "real-time" negotiation and chat sessions. In addition, three on-campus research facilities have access to the local area network (LAN) which includes computer workstations with networked access to CD-ROMs, an OPAC, various indexes, and desktop publishing programs.

Class Assignment

Integrated into the Department of Modern Languages in 1971, the English as a Second Language program provides instruction at several levels: intensive, intermediate, and advanced. The work with on-line research materials, and with corporate research in particular, takes place in the advanced level course, Advanced English Composition and Introductory Business Communications. This course is designed to improve writing skills and includes instruction in the fundamentals of business letter and document writing. Students are encouraged to have a CompuServe account and are required to have an Internet and e-mail account.

The centerpiece of the course is the corporate research project which is a requirement and constitutes 25% of the final course grade. This project is designed to teach students to conduct meetings, write a strategic plan, and prepare, present and defend their conclusions and recommendations. A team contract is also required. Through this project, students learn to use on-line research databases, prepare PowerPoint slides to accompany their final oral presentation, and to use EXCEL, ACCESS, and LOTUS.

During the Spring 1996 Semester, ESL students selected their company, and then they were put on the Internet and connected to the business website from the University of North Carolina at Charlotte in order to access stock prices, corporate home pages, and industry profiles to be incorporated into their formal reports. Students learned to bookmark useful websites and, with the help of the ESL instructor, worked to shape the drafts of their reports. These drafts were then reviewed by other faculty, library personnel, and Career Services staff. The students' work was then published by the Career Services center and made available on campus though the Thunderbird website and through the Thunderbird Forum on CompuServe.

During the Spring 1996 semester, three groups were formed for this corporate research project. Each group consisted of seven to ten ESL students; assignments within each group were determined by the students, with input from the instructor. The papers averaged from 120 to 140 pages in length and included all requirements of a formal report, i.e., an executive summary, table of contents, introduction, body, conclusions and recommendations, analysis of the strengths, weaknesses, opportunities and threats of a company and the fit of the company within an industry, and a detailed annotated bibliography.

CREATION OF THE COURSE-SPECIFIC WEBSITE

Background

The University of North Carolina at Charlotte is one of the newest members of the University of North Carolina System and is accredited by the Southern Association of Colleges and Schools. It is a comprehensive, regional university, granting bachelors and masters degrees; it has been approved to grant doctoral degrees. As of Fall, 1995, enrollment was 15,948 students. The Belk College of Business Administration is accredited by the American Assembly of Collegiate Schools of Business and grants bachelors and masters degrees. As of Fall, 1995, enrollment was 2,367 undergraduate students and 327 graduate students.

J. Murrey Atkins Library is the main library on the UNC Charlotte campus. As of Fall, 1995, it houses 601,902 volumes, over 3,000 periodical subscriptions, and over 1 million microforms. The Reference Unit consists of 10 librarians, approximately 30,000 volumes, 14 end-user workstations, and two Internet terminals. Two of the reference librarians are business specialists; both have a second advanced degree in a business-related field.

Course-Based Website

The international business subject specialist provides library instruction for both domestic and international business classes. For several years she has provided library instruction for undergraduate and MBA-level management classes (taught by the same instructor) that required students to analyze a company and its industry, a standard assignment found in many collegiate schools of business. Library instruction for these classes followed the traditional format of providing a written bibliography of sources and a demonstration of various electronic sources, including *General BusinessFile ASAP*, and *Dow Jones News/Retrieval*. *General BusinessFile ASAP* and *Dow Jones News/Retrieval* are accessed via the Internet; *Compact Disclosure* is available on the library's local area network.

In 1995, the Internet was integrated into library instruction. More and more reference librarians are using the Internet as a library instruction tool in a variety of ways.[1] The librarians in the Reference Unit are not exceptions. Every reference librarian has access to the Internet and has training in writing home pages and mounting websites. As more and more information became available via the Internet and the UNC Charlotte campus became "wired" with Internet access in the computer labs, the international business subject specialist created a website which included hot links to sources of U.S. business information, including stock prices, corporate home pages, industry statistics, and business news sources. The management professor was invited to a demonstration, agreed to the sources, their arrangement on the website, and to a format for citing Internet sources in the required bibliography. The other business subject specialist then became webmaster and named the website "Internet Sources for U.S. Corporate, Industrial, and Economic Information" (URL: http://library.uncc.edu/lis/library/services/reference/usbus/buselec.htm). The website was made accessible from the Reference Unit's home page.

During the one-hour library instruction session, the international business subject specialist demonstrated the traditional electronic sources (e.g., *Compact Disclosure*) and gave a brief overview of the Internet (e.g., logging on, URLs, hot links, etc.) and demonstrated the course-specific website. A printed handout of Internet "basics" was also distributed to students.

To evaluate the effectiveness of the library instruction for theses classes, citation analysis has been employed for several semesters. Citation analysis is a well-known method of evaluating the effectiveness of library instruction.[2] At the end of each semester the instructor provided the librarian with the bibliographies from one of the class sections. The librarian checked the citations in the students' bibliographies against both the printed handout and the electronic sources to ascertain whether they were using sources suggested by the librarian and to see if there were any additional sources that the students found that could be added to the website.

At UNC Charlotte an analysis of the bibliographies submitted by the students in the graduate management course during the Spring 1996 semester indicated that of the 37 papers submitted, students used Internet sources in 12 papers. The types of Internet sites accessed were corporate home pages, U.S. government websites, industry trade association home pages, *PR Newswire*, and electronic trade journals. Of the remaining 25 papers, 18 used other electronic sources such as *Dow Jones New/Retrieval*, *ProQuest* (available at the local public library), *General BusinessFile ASAP*, and *Compustat* (available in the business computer labs).

EFFECTIVENESS OF THE WEBSITE

Citation Analysis of ESL Students' Bibliographies

At Thunderbird, citation analysis of the bibliographies demonstrated that all three groups used references taken from the Internet. Of the 65 bibliographical entries included, 21 (or about 32%) came directly from Internet sources. The types of websites accessed included corporate home pages, government websites, industry and trade home pages, financial reports, and on-line publications. Other electronic sources cited were from *NEXIS, ABI Inform, CompuServe Library and Forums, ProQuest Business Dateline, Dow Jones News/Retrieval*, and *Compustat.*

Qualitative Differences in ESL Students' Projects

At Thunderbird the use of Internet sources made the data in the reports more timely, excited the ESL students, and involved them in the process of creating documents that would be seen as current and relevant. The process of teaching students to do on-line searches and of involving business research specialists in the writing process taught students to see librarians and other information specialists as central to the graduate school learning process. The collaboration and mentoring made these projects the most sophisticated to date, including very savvy analyses of "corporate fit," of corporate competitiveness, and of corporate culture. They clearly demonstrated that the use of up-to-date, cutting-edge material in the research process resulted in a corporate report that is useful for its discussions of the industry, affiliates, organizational structure, human resource management, management styles and policies, corporate missions, marketing and competition, financial information, corporate reengineering, and changes in the corporate paradigm.

CONCLUSION

Teaching students to use the latest in computer-based communication technology is of paramount importance in this globally networked international business community. At the university level, some 68% of the faculty recently polled by the *Business Communication Quarterly* require their students to use computer software and hardware to complete some writing assignments. Sixty percent of those surveyed covered additional topics with multimedia presentations. Some of those surveyed also indicated that they use e-mail and the Internet to provide instruction to their students.[3] All of these numbers point to the need for instructors and librarians to continue to collaborate to encourage the use of electronic research tools, electronic transmission of assignments and evaluation feedback to parallel the merging trend toward the paperless office, computer networks, and e-mail.

In another recent article in *Business Communication Quarterly*, the incorporation of research methods into the business communication course was discussed. The authors also contended that the teaching of research techniques " . . . should be an integrated, on-going part of basic courses requiring the conducting and sharing of research-based data."[4]

This type of research teaches ESL students to value management and communication research, to make informed decisions within and beyond corporate boundaries, to analyze and adapt to a given audience, and to gather, synthesize and analyze data from multiple sources with multiple points of view. Teaching ESL students to use the Internet as a research tool encourages them to become life-long learners and to develop and hone skills in conducting research as part of their regular work, not as a "one-time" project requirement. This interactivity also illustrates to instructors that full participation by students drives an authentic dialogue in the classroom and encourages stimulating and challenging discussions, all of which build the students' communication and research skills.

The use of information technology and the integration of this technology into the curriculum provides expanded learning opportunities for students[5] and research does indicate that such integration of technology will create a better and more positive learning environment.

ENDNOTES

1. See Glorianna St. Clair and Rose Mary Margrill, "Undergraduate Term Paper Citations," *College & Research Library News* no. 1 (January 1990): 25-28, and Margaret Sylvia and Marcella Lesher, "What Journals Do Psychology Graduate Students Need? A Citation Analysis of Thesis References," *College and Research Libraries* 56 (July 1995): 313-318.

2. See Carl Braun, "The Use of Web Pages for Active Learning," *Business &
Finance Division Bulletin* no. 102 (Spring 1996): 37-42, and Pablo Martin de Ho-
lan and Veronica Kisfalvi, "Internet in the Business Classroom," *Business & Finance Division Bulletin* no. 102 (Spring 1996): 51-56.

3. Zane Quible and Eric Ray, "Using the Internet in Written Business Communication," *Business Communication Quarterly* no. 4 (December 1995): 11-16.

4. Sandra Nelson, Douglas C. Smith, Keneth R. Mayer, and William Galle,
"The Status of Computer Use in Business Communication Instruction," *Business
Communication Quarterly* no. 4 (December 1995): 17.

5. Linda Loehr, "An Integrated Approach to Introducing Research Methods in
Required Business and Technical Writing Courses" *Business Communication
Quarterly* no. 4 (December 1995): 25-27.

Developing an Internet Site
for School Business Officials:
Benefits
of a Reference Librarian-External User
Partnership

Katherine M. Shelfer
Chase W. Crawford

SUMMARY. An external user and an academic business reference librarian collaborated to identify useful Internet resources for members of the Association of School Business Officials (ASBO). The patron provided computer skills and knowledge of the information needs of school business officials. The librarian provided knowledge of resources and access to the Internet. This service commitment to an "outsider" who was not part of the primary user population directly improved the librarian's working relationships with her primary user population and improved her ability to serve her professional association. She also gained understanding of the information needs and changing role of school business officials. This paper describes the collaborative effort and the results, and focuses on the development process used to create an Internet site. *[Article copies available for a fee from The Haworth Document Delivery Service: 1-800-342-9678. E-mail address: getinfo@haworth.com]*

Katherine M. Shelfer is affiliated with the Strozier Library, The Florida State University, Tallahassee, FL. Chase W. Crawford is affiliated with the Florida Department of Education, Tallahassee, FL.

[Haworth co-indexing entry note]: "Developing an Internet Site for School Business Officials: Benefits of a Reference Librarian-External User Partnership." Shelfer, Katherine M. and Chase W. Crawford. Co-published simultaneously in *The Reference Librarian* (The Haworth Press, Inc.) No. 58, 1997, pp. 13-26; and: *Business Reference Services and Sources: How End Users and Librarians Work Together* (ed: Katherine M. Shelfer) The Haworth Press, Inc., 1997, pp. 13-26. Single or multiple copies of this article are available for a fee from The Haworth Document Delivery Service [1-800-342-9678, 9:00 a.m. - 5:00 p.m. (EST). E-mail address: getinfo@haworth.com].

13

INTRODUCTION

Academic business reference librarians are charged with supporting the research and teaching missions of the academic institution by which they are employed. This generally means that they provide services which focus on the needs of the institution's faculty, students and staff–the primary user population. Fiscal restrictions and staffing limitations make it tempting to provide only "bare bones" service to "outsiders," those individuals who are not obviously a part of the primary user population. Service policies vary for external users ("Reference," 1993). However, reference librarians are not omniscient. Working relationships often exist between members of the general public and members of the academic institution which are not readily apparent to the reference librarian. Providing extended business reference services to "outsiders" may at times have unexpected rewards and result in improved service to the primary user population.

In order to effectively support research and teaching, academic business reference librarians attempt to maintain current awareness of available resources. Exploration of the Internet is beneficial because it results in the identification of additional useful resources and provides the librarian with an awareness of the research techniques available to end-users who are searching the Internet. The process is very time-consuming, however, because of the explosion of Internet sites. Business reference librarians may fail to recognize potentially useful Internet resources in some research areas simply because they are not able to focus equal effort on every aspect of business. Once Internet resources are identified, the librarian must then solve the problem of providing access to them. Day and Armstrong (1996) reported on the efforts of librarians to assist faculty when their needs did not match their technical abilities. In addition to individualized and group instruction, access may include print and electronic resource guides, the library's catalog, and/or the library's homepage, but each of these solutions requires considerable time and effort to develop and maintain.

Therefore, efforts to identify appropriate Internet business resources and make them available to researchers are more likely to be successful when the efforts are shared by librarians and other stakeholders–those who (1) have an interest in identifying and providing access to appropriate Internet resources, and (2) are most likely to recognize the utility of a site. This paper describes the process and the successful outcomes of one such collaborative effort between a librarian and an "outsider" library patron which resulted in a direct improvement of services to the primary user population.

BACKGROUND

At the Association of School Business Officials (ASBO) conference in Seattle in October 1994, the Microsoft education marketing representative for the Pacific Northwest discussed the Internet briefly in two of his presentations. This overview stimulated the interest of Dr. Chase Crawford, an official with the Florida Department of Education, who had a great deal of experience working with computers. He was intensely interested in the potential of the Internet to provide financial and other resources to school business officials, but two factors hindered his efforts. First, there was no access to the Internet in his office, and very restricted access to the Internet elsewhere in the Florida Department of Education, his place of employment. Also, while he was able to obtain some books on the Internet, he had no experience in identifying and filtering Internet sites, or in comparing them to existing print and electronic resources. Therefore, he contacted the business reference librarian at the Florida State University (FSU) to request access and assistance.

At the time of the initial request, there was only one computer with public Internet access on the FSU campus–it was a gift of FSU's Congress of Graduate Students (COGS) intended for use by both library staff and patrons. The keyboard and monitor faced the staff on the side counter of the U-shaped reference desk, so anyone who wanted to use it had to request permission to work on the staff side of the counter. Despite a sign posted on the side of the monitor, few patrons used it.

The librarian had an understanding of evolving Internet capabilities. She was aware of print and traditional fee-based information sources, so she was able to compare/contrast the quality and depth of the Internet information against standard resources. Providentially, the business librarian wore multiple hats. She was the library's fledgling gopher master, resident Internet instructor, and in charge of computer equipment for the reference department. She had taught several uncompensated weekend workshops for COGS which had resulted in the donation of the system. This gave her some control over its use. She wanted the COGS equipment to be used by the public.

Access by nonaffiliated patrons to extensive reference services has generated much debate. Jansen (1993) pointed out that external users are a fact of life. Russell, Robison and Prather (1989) reported on a survey of external users in urban university libraries, and Best-Nichols (1993) examined the issue of access to academic libraries by external users in North Carolina. Therefore, when the patron requested her assistance, the business reference librarian faced a dilemma. If she chose to provide him with access and instruction, it would be time-consuming. It would reduce the time and attention available to the primary user population. Severe staff shortages had resulted in some staff disgruntlement with "outsiders," which was not unusual, according to Verhoeven, Cooksey and Hand (1996). However, the business reference librarian understood the conditions which hindered this patron's ability to gain access to the equipment and information elsewhere, so she elected to provide the services he requested. In order to minimize potential resistance of other staff to this level of service to an "outsider," particularly one who would be working on the staff side of the reference desk, she suggested that he use the terminal on the nights and weekends when she was the (only) librarian on duty in the department. This would allow her to provide him with maximum assistance while meeting minimum resistance from other staff. In Spring 1995, the patron and the librarian began working together and sharing information on a weekly basis.

The patron was eager to learn. Within a few months he found access to the Internet at his place of employment and expanded the amount of time he was able to spend on the process away from the library. The librarian served as a reader's advisor, recommending additional books and periodicals about the Internet which the patron obtained and read, often sharing what he learned. Each challenged the other to identify core finance and investments sites which meet the needs of ASBO members. As weeks passed, telephone discussions and e-mail replaced the regular weekly meetings, and occasional meetings became the norm.

At the ASBO Conference in Nashville in October 1995, the patron presented a 40-page handout abstracting several hundred Internet sites, both gopher and web, which were organized into about 15 categories. There was a general air of excitement about the presentations. A computer and ISDN line were provided by Bell South which permitted a large-screen demonstration of many of these sites to about 125 attendees.

At the ASBO Conference in Philadelphia in November 1996, the patron expanded his efforts and presented five hands-on sessions on the Internet. Three sessions were for beginners, with 150, 125, and 75 participants, respectively. One session was for 75 intermediate-level users on searching techniques, and one was for 50 intermediate-level users with no specific topic advertised. All sessions used Pentium, Windows 95 CPUs networked to a file server provided by EDUNET, Inc. of Pittsburgh, with a T-1 line to an AT&T service center. Additional time was made available to attendees each day to browse the Internet.

The patron used his Internet research and feedback from attendees at the ASBO conferences to develop a web site. This process introduced the librarian to other types of information needs of school business officials. It also provided her with an opportunity to observe the process of creating a web site for use by a target population.

DESIGNING THE WEB SITE

The arrangement of the site for school business officials is needs-based. The first design consideration was to target member needs rather than to adhere to any particular organizational structure or layout scheme. The patron began by defining the information needs of school business officials. He then listed information on the homepage in priority order by the expected amount of use (see Figure 1). The librarian found this approach visually ugly and thought that the categories were unbalanced. When she objected, she learned that the patron's discussions with ASBO members at the conferences demonstrated a clear preference for access to the most heavily used information regardless of provenance or name recognition.

She also learned that the information needs of school business officials extend far beyond finance or investment information. School business officials handle the "business" or non-instructional part of the daily operations of schools. Managing cash flow is a critical component of the workload, but it is not the only one. Sielke (1995) pointed out that the duties of school business officials encompass technical, human relations and conceptual areas. Stevenson and Warren (1996) discussed the major shifts in the business official's role and the importance of current awareness of social issues, education alternatives, and technology. They believe that school business officials must become entrepreneurial to be effective. According to Nowakowski and Schneider (1996), school business officials can save districts money or increase revenue through sound financial practices, planning, grantsmanship, and knowledge of accounting, tax, legal and legislative, and insurance and risk management information, purchasing practices, technology, transportation, food service, current news and demographics.

Therefore, the primary resources in "A School Business Official's Pathfinder" are based on the typical organization of the non-instructional part of a school system's staff. These were arranged in three (and later, four) categories:

I. Government resources, legal and legislative resources, Internet security, funds transfer, banks, investment resources, taxes, accountants' resources, and risk management and insurance.

II. Internet information, technology hardware and software, technology publications, publication services, newspapers, broadcast and cable media, and other publications.

III. Health resources, human resources, associations, commercial services, food service, transportation, and miscellaneous.

A fourth category, developed during the course of the project, was designed to allow users to find information on the Internet. Links allow researchers to locate (1) information on this web site using the Harvest search engine from the University of Colorado; (2) business information on the Internet through web catalogs, or directories, of business information resources; and (3) any kind of information on the Internet using general catalogs or search engines.

Separate files were created for each category to reduce the time spent in updating and reformatting the site. The following sections describe the criteria for resource selection:

Accountants' Resources

Schools and school systems must comply with current financial and managerial accounting practices, as well as with internal auditing practices appropriate to entities which use public funds. Accounting resources include (1) links to the web sites of various large accounting firms; (2) regional and national professional associations; and (3) sites which identify discussion lists, documents and working papers.

Banks

Economic data provided by Federal Reserve Banks are included in this category. Web sites of national and regional banks, credit unions, and credit card issuers describe services appropriate for school systems and school system employees. Sites produced by financial institutions describe types of accounts available, interest rates for accounts and certificates of deposit, and information on various credit cards. Associations and consortia of financial service providers, universities and government agencies provide working papers and updates on research efforts, such as interbank technical projects, so a few such links are included.

Commercial Internet Resources

The commercial sites of greatest interest are those which offer information and insights into electronic commerce designed to allow efficient interaction between customers, suppliers and development partners in order to speed time to market and reduce the cost of doing business.

FIGURE 1

WELCOME TO

A SCHOOL BUSINESS OFFICIAL'S

INTERNET PATHFINDER

The information available on the Internet of interest to school business staff is classified into the following bracketed topics, which also serve as a table of contents for this Web site. These topical listings will link you to the Web pages identifying the Internet sites on each topic.

FOR ACCOUNTING, BUDGETING, LEGAL, LEGISLATIVE, SCHOOL FINANCE, AND SIMILAR AREAS OF INTEREST
[GOVERNMENT RESOURCES] * [LEGAL AND LEGISLATIVE RESOURCES]
[INTERNET SECURITY] * [TRANSFERRING FUNDS] * [BANKS] * [INVESTMENT RESOURCES]
[TAXES] * [ACCOUNTANTS' RESOURCES] * [RISK MANAGEMENT AND INSURANCE]

FOR TECHNOLOGY, INFORMATION SYSTEMS, GENERAL INFORMATION, AND SIMILAR AREAS OF INTEREST
[INTERNET INFORMATION] * [TECHNOLOGY HARDWARE AND SOFTWARE]
[TECHNOLOGY PUBLICATIONS] * [PUBLICATIONS SERVICES]
[NEWSPAPERS] * [BROADCAST AND CABLE MEDIA] * [OTHER PUBLICATIONS]

FOR ALL OTHER AREAS OF INTEREST
[HEALTH RESOURCES] * [HUMAN RESOURCES] * [ASSOCIATIONS]
[ASBOI EXHIBITORS] NEW! * [AASA EXHIBITORS] NEW! * [COMMERCIAL]
[FOOD SERVICE] * [TRANSPORTATION] * [MISCELLANEOUS]

HOW TO FIND INFORMATION ON THE INTERNET
[FINDING INFORMATION ON A SCHOOL BUSINESS OFFICIAL'S WEB SITE] NEW!
[FINDING BUSINESS INFORMATION ON THE INTERNET]
[FINDING ANY KIND OF INFORMATION ON THE INTERNET]

The contributors to the Internet sites identified in the attachments to this homepage make no guarantees as to the accuracy, currency, content, or quality of any information or services provided by such sites or any additional sites you reach from these sites.

This page has been accessed 3312 times. This page last revised February 21, 1997. ©

Return to FIRN home page.

Send your suggestions for changes, questions, or other comments to CRAWFOCW@MAIL.FIRN.EDU

Manufacturers catalogs, package tracking services, and classified lists of goods and services available for purchase are examples of resources which fit this category.

Finding Any Kind of Information on the Internet

Links to lists of business resources, business news services, business magazines, stocks and stock reports, personal finance, Federal information (FEDWORLD), and Internet finding aids or indexes including search engine directories, meta search engines, and Internic finding aids are included in this category. The goal is to provide resources which will speed access to relevant information accessed via the Internet.

Finding Business Information on the Internet

Appropriate resources in this category are (1) links to sites with documents which provide information needed by school business officials; (2) links to lists of business resources, primarily those compiled by business librarians; (3) links to sites of financial information providers such as Hoovers and Babson College; and (4) monitoring services for Internet financial services. Interesting and experimental sites would also be included here, but only as carefully chosen examples of the Internet's potential. In this way, school business officials will be able to keep up with the Internet without prolonged "surfing."

Government Resources in Business

Composite sites such as STAT-USA, the Census, the Bureau of Economic Analysis, Labor and the Bureau of Labor Statistics provide economic and demographic data. Documents related to the National Information Infrastructure (NII) initiative and other initiatives affecting school systems are placed in this section. The FEDWORLD site fits as well.

Investment Resources

School business officials manage the money. They need access to the most current financial and investment resources available. Links to stock exchanges that provide information about companies listed on the exchange, equity options and derivative products, daily market summaries and customized research services are placed in this section. Links to investment services which present stock charts, quote services, business news, insurance ratings services, and quotes on U.S. Treasury securities fit here as well. This section must provide practical business/investment information which is very current and rapidly accessed. Because it is a large section, it is divided into several components: information; mutual funds; corporate information; commodities; investment banks; brokers; miscellaneous; and Usenet.

Legal and Legislative

The *U.S. Code of Federal Regulations*, The *Catalog of Federal Domestic Assistance*, the *Federal Register*, and the Thomas Legislative Information Service provide information related to federal grants, regulations, and legislative initiatives which apply to school systems. Topics related to business law also fit into this category.

Newspapers

The *Chronicle of Higher Education* (which appears every Tuesday at noon), *USA Today*, CNN, and other major newspapers and newspaper-like services provide current information on lead news stories, money, politics, sports, technology, and the weather. ASBO members are very busy and have very little time to read general papers. Internet services listed in this category must put only the most significant information at their fingertips without unnecessary frills that delay access to the information.

Other Publications

The *Journal of Finance* as well as a number of general interest publications (e.g., *Time*, *Money*, and *Fortune*) fit into this category, as do full-text reference works such as the *Thomas Register of American Manufacturers*.

Publication Services

Commercial news services and booksellers are listed in this section. Fee-based on-line information services which provide extensive full-text legal, news and business information (e.g., LEXIS-NEXIS) are also linked in this section, as are bibliographic services (e.g., Uncover) which provide free abstract searching and document delivery services.

Internet Security

School business officials need to have access to information related to electronic transactions and Internet commerce, and they rightly fear computer break-ins. They need direct access to the latest information on Internet security. Sites listed here must include substantial, current, technical information on software/protocols. Other helpful sites are those which describe potential solutions for common problems.

Taxes

The U.S. Tax Code On-Line provides complete access in a number of searching combinations to the IRS Code, Title 26 (26 USC) (http://www.fourmilab.ch/ustax/ustax.html). Tax forms, and information on state and local taxes fit into this section.

Technology Hardware and Software

Technology sites are fluid and can be difficult to annotate, but technology information is important. Information on computers and telecommunications hardware and software is especially important. Link to companies which provide goods/services under federal, state and local contracts are useful. Many company sites provide product catalogs including specifications for components and system packages, pricing information, benchmarks, reviews, advice, and direct e-mail to technical support and sales staff. This is especially important as school systems update their wiring and telecommunications capabilities.

Transferring Funds

There are several entities which have teamed up to provide secure transmission of credit card information and funds transfer. One example is CyberCash, described by Freeman (1996), which provides instant verifications. There a link to DigiCash, which works with smart cards, security and electronic payments systems, and links to Visa and MasterCard. Banks are beginning to enter the picture with rudimentary services such as access to account information, funds transfer and bill-paying services. The Automated Clearinghouse (ACH) has connected banks since the mid-1970s, and certainly belongs in this group.

Transportation

The need for transportation information is related to yellow school buses, urban transportation systems, suppliers, pupil transportation web sites, classified advertising, industry statistics, and association events. The linked pages provide access to chat rooms, *Federal Register* rulemakings, industry and academic research and statistics. *School Transportation News*, a monthly magazine with a circulation of over 18,000, is included. This title reports on school bus transportation news, industry contacts, and industry data. Information which can be gathered from this section covers maintenance, outsourcing and other contractual arrangements, insurance and risk management, lists of available publications, and much more.

MAKING THE WEB SITE AVAILABLE

Once the site was configured and the programming complete on the initial version, technical problems and a staff emergency prevented the patron from loading the finished product on the designated server housed at the Florida Information Resource Network (FIRN) server. The librarian had, with the assistance of the patron, begun creation of a "Business Webrary" site. As a result, she was able to load the patron's site into her site as a sub-directory. This made it available to the librarian's primary user population through links from the university's home page as well as to school business officials who learned of it. Once the site was loaded on FIRN (http://www.firn.edu/~asbo/asbo.html), the librarian continued her involvement as a back-up site. Periodically, the patron visits the library and uploads the new version directly into the librarian's sub-directory. This process allows both collaborators to identify and resolve new technical issues which occur when a site is customized for a particular server and reloaded on a separate server. The learning continues, and it benefits all stakeholders. The official ASBO site (http://www.asbointl.org) does not provide links to resource lists of this nature, so this page, discussed and circulated at conferences, provides a very real service to ASBO members. It was named "A School Business Official's Internet Pathfinder" so that if it does become an "official" link, the acronym ASBO can easily be added to the page.

BENEFITS TO THE LIBRARIAN

Due in part to expertise gained in this project, the librarian was asked to serve on the library's catalog and Internet menu-planning committees, the library's distance education committee, and a consortium committee evaluating on-line databases.

Even though the patron's knowledge and abilities soon out-paced the librarian's, he continued his support of her efforts. Each step of the process took countless hours for the patron, but he willingly summarized the high points and taught them to the librarian in only a fraction of that time. For example, when it became apparent from feedback that users wanted a way to locate a link on the site without knowing its category, the patron developed a composite alphabetical index to all the sites listed in each category.

The patron went on to evaluate search engines which could be used to locate key words appearing in any of the files in the site. He selected the Harvest software from the University of Colorado. When he next met with the librarian, he described the evaluation process and his reasons for selecting this software, again in only minutes.

The patron explained terminology which the librarian encountered in her reading. This made it possible to understand articles, such as Spangler's (1996), which discussed Common Gateway Interface (CGI) scripts and various softwares. When the patron decided to evaluate usage of the site, he worked with FIRN to establish a counter on each of the "pages." This counter was programmed to count the number of "hits" or the number of times the page was accessed. He demonstrated this counter and the programming it required to the librarian. Armed with this new information, the librarian requested one for her home page, only to learn that such a counter would not be provided on a university server. Shortly thereafter, the librarian wrote a proposal for a library local area network. She hopes to mount counters once the local server has been configured.

Creating the html script for the site was time-consuming, so the patron explored and tested various authoring softwares. Again, he summarized his findings for the librarian. He taught the librarian how to write html scripts and how to build tables, and provided her with templates for use in her own web site. Each of these skills would have taken the librarian untold hours to master alone, but the patron as teacher summarized the important points, demonstrated each step, and willingly provided examples and templates.

BENEFITS TO THE PRIMARY USER POPULATION

The patron provided the librarian with new opportunities to serve her primary user population. He contacted several faculty members in FSU's finance department, and audited several classes. He initiated, scheduled, and team-taught personal investments classes with the librarian in which they demonstrated a combination of print and electronic library and Internet resources. When other faculty members in the Finance and Hospitality departments heard about the classes, they scheduled similar class instruction for senior management, international hospitality management and entrepreneurship which the librarian taught solo. These faculty voluntarily provided information on their different approaches to similar case analysis assignments. Several were instrumental in obtaining a new computer for the librarian's office in the College of Business!

The librarian had previously tried many ways to interest faculty in research instruction for their students. She had tried individual mailings, e-mail to faculty lists, announcements in university newsletters and even advertisements in student newspapers. Nothing had worked very well. She provided instruction on a regular basis for certain teaching assistants and a few faculty, but very few tenured faculty had requested instruction for their students. This one "outsider" patron was able to reach three members of the Finance faculty, and two members of the Hospitality department were then reached by word-of-mouth. Each faculty member later requested that this type of research instruction be provided for his/her classes on a standing basis.

Students who received the instruction actively sought out the librarian for additional information and clarification. In many cases, they came to the reference desk having already obtained basic information covered in the classes. A few groups of students e-mailed the librarian to schedule appointments and to request e-mail reference assistance with selecting topics and resources. The librarian began to find her work much more stimulating and enjoyable as a result.

During the process, the librarian used her new-found skills to create a web site of business resources. She was able to integrate her knowledge of the research needs of school business officials into graduate courses in government documents and business resources which she taught in FSU's library school in 1995-1997. Knowledge and skills gained through this collaborative effort proved to be very helpful to the librarian when, in 1996, the Publications Committee that she chaired for the American Library Association, Reference and User Services, Business References and Services Section (ALA/RUSA/BRASS) was charged with the creation of a web site for BRASS.

CONCLUSION

The librarian and the "outsider" built a mutually beneficial working relationship which served both their primary user populations. The "outsider" generated considerable goodwill and additional bibliographic instruction opportunities for the librarian. Both collaborators prepared professional papers. The "outsider" made several presentations at national conferences, and the librarian used her knowledge to oversee creation of a web site for her professional association. Both gained needed skills and confidence in using the Internet for research. In this case, the librarian's decision to extend service beyond the "bare bones" clearly resulted in a direct gain to the library's primary user population.

REFERENCES

Best-Nichols, Barbara. "Community Use of Tax-Supported Libraries in North Carolina system: Is Unlimited Access a Right?" *North Carolina Libraries* 51, 120-5, Fall 1993.

Day, Pam A. And Kimberly L. Armstrong. "Librarians, Faculty and the Internet: Developing a New Information Partnership." *Computers in Libraries* 16,5, 56-58, May 1996.

Freeman, Eva. "How to Move E-Cash Around the Internet." *Datamation* 42,16, 58-62, October 1996.

Jansen, Lloyd M. "Welcome or Not, Here They Come: Unaffiliated Users of Academic Libraries." *Reference Services Review* 21,1 7-14, 1993.

Nowakowski, Ben C. And Robert Schneider. "A Good Business Manager Can Save You Money." *School Business Affairs* 62,7, 43-44, July 1996.

"Reference Policies for Primary Users and Others." *Information Bulletin* (Western Association of Map Libraries) 25, 48-51, Nov. 1993.

Russell, Ralph E., Carolyn Love Robison and James E. Prather. "External Access to Academic Libraries." *Southeastern Librarian* 39, 15-8, Winter 1989.

Sielke, Catherine C. "More than a Number Cruncher: The Business Administrator's Changing Role." *School Business Affairs* 61,6, 33-37, June 1995.

Spangler, Todd. "Search and Sort Your Web." [Sidebar to "Content and Collaboration"]. *PC Magazine* 15,8, 142, April 23, 1996.

Stevenson, Kenneth R. and Elizabeth Warren. "Weathering the Future: The Changing Role of the School Business Official." *School Business Affairs* 62,4, 35-38, April 1996.

Verhoeven, Stanley M., Elizabeth B. Cooksey and Carol A. Hand. "The Disproportionate Use of Reference Desk Services by External Users at an Urban University Library." *RQ* 35, 392-7, Spring 1996.

Company Information
on the World Wide Web:
Using Corporate Home Pages
to Supplement
Traditional Business Resources

Joseph A. LaRose

SUMMARY. Used in conjunction with more traditional business reference resources, the World Wide Web can help fill out a company's picture. Corporate Web presences may range from single-page company descriptions to multi-layered sites that take fuller advantage of the Web's immense capacity and interactive nature. Maintained primarily to promote and advertise a company's products and services, company sites often contain information on company history, employment opportunities, news, and company philosophy. They can reveal a great deal about a company's image and can serve as a case study of its marketing strategy. Sometimes information about a particular company can be found on the Web and in no other library resource.

This article describes items typically found in corporate Web sites that complement what is contained in a library's more traditional business resources. In addition, it recommends some business-related directories on the Web and gives tips for using Web search en-

Joseph A. LaRose is Assistant Professor of Bibliography and Reference Librarian, Bierce Library, The University of Akron, Akron, OH 44325-1709. E-mail: jl@uakron.edu

[Haworth co-indexing entry note]: "Company Information on the World Wide Web: Using Corporate Home Pages to Supplement Traditional Business Resources." LaRose, Joseph A. Co-published simultaneously in *The Reference Librarian* (The Haworth Press, Inc.) No. 58, 1997, pp. 27-39; and: *Business Reference Services and Sources: How End Users and Librarians Work Together* (ed: Katherine M. Shelfer) The Haworth Press, Inc., 1997, pp. 27-39. Single or multiple copies of this article are available for a fee from The Haworth Document Delivery Service [1-800-342-9678, 9:00 a.m. - 5:00 p.m. (EST). E-mail address: getinfo@haworth.com].

27

gines to find company home pages. *[Article copies available for a fee from The Haworth Document Delivery Service: 1-800-342-9678. E-mail address: getinfo@haworth.com]*

Think of business reference and you might think of standard resources like *Moody's Manuals, Ward's Business Directory, ValueLine Investment Survey,* and *Compact Disclosure.* Factual and unbiased, they are trusted sources of information on a company's finances, industry position, size, stock, and location. Now consider another resource, the World Wide Web, with its thousands of corporate and entrepreneurial home pages. What business information is contained therein? Can it help answer the business-related questions typically asked by library patrons?

Used in conjunction with more traditional business reference resources, the World Wide Web can help fill out a company's picture. Corporate Web presences may range from single-page company descriptions to multi-layered sites that take fuller advantage of the Web's immense capacity and interactive nature. Maintained primarily to promote and advertise a company's products and services, company sites often contain information on company history, employment opportunities, news, and company philosophy. They can reveal a great deal about a company's image and can serve as a case study of its marketing strategy.

This article describes items typically found in corporate Web sites that complement what is contained in a library's more traditional business resources. In addition, it recommends some business-related directories on the Web and gives tips for using Web search engines to find company home pages.

WHAT COMPANIES ARE ON THE WEB?

Insofar as having a Web presence is now almost expected in the world of big business, most Fortune 500 companies, public corporations, and the largest companies have home pages on the Web. Often used as launching places for an array of interactive features–designed to promote the company as well as to sell its products–the sites for large corporations such as IBM, McDonald's, Black & Decker, and AT&T, are among the most sophisticated on the Web.

However, having a Web site is by no means limited to the largest companies, nor does a site have to be fancy. With a range of professional Web-services providers who can design and maintain a company's site at all cost-levels, more and more smaller companies of all sizes–from medium to small firms down to sole proprietorships run from the home–are establishing pages on the Web to advertise, market, and sell their products or services. While many of the smaller companies utilize high-end graphics in their Web presences, some company's pages are merely a single page of text. Whatever degree of sophistication used, businesses of all sizes are establishing presences on the Web by the score. An indication of this is the jump in registered commercial domains (.com) from 29,000 as of December 31, 1994 to 170,000 as of January 5, 1996, an increase of 586%.[1] It is estimated that the commercial sector now accounts for more than three-fourths of all registered Internet addresses.[2]

PART ONE:
WHAT INFORMATION IS USEFUL FOR REFERENCE?

Certainly, not everything found at a company's site will be useful at the reference desk. Since a corporate Web site exists primarily for advertising and promotion, we must consider the company's own interests when evaluating the information we find. Moreover, company Web sites vary greatly in size and content. Nevertheless, a great deal of information is commonly found—in the sites of giant corporations down to the smallest of companies—that can supplement what is found in the more objective business resources. The following list categorizes some useful information typically found.

Product Information. With its unlimited capacity and hyper-text linking abilities, the Web allows companies to provide in-depth product information. Some companies include catalog-listings of their entire lines. For example, 3M Corporation (*http://www.mmm.com*) provides an easy-to-browse list of links to specific information about hundreds of its products; similarly, Fiat has a virtual showroom with photographs and specifics about its entire automobile line (*http:/www.fiat.com*). One may find interesting facts about products—as in the Ben & Jerry company's description of which percentages of its sorbet-bound strawberries and raspberries are organic (*http://www.benjerry.com*)—or browse impartial evaluations through links to the texts of product reviews. It is not uncommon to find, such as in the sites for Budweiser (*http://www.budweiser.com*) and Integrated Systems Research Corporation (*http://www.access.digex.net/~rheckart/*), links to other sites that house educational materials about a company's product, technology, or industry.

News. The Web can be a good place to find out about a company's current developments. Since a site can be updated at a moment's notice, companies often take advantage of their Web presence to make announcements. Indeed, sites for larger companies commonly include a section labeled "News," containing press releases. Prepared by a company, a press release typically gives information about new products, partnerships, programs, awards, and employees. Sometimes links to articles in magazines and newspapers about the company are provided. For an example of a well-maintained news page, see 3Com's "What's New at 3Com" (*http://www.3com.com*).

Company History. The history of a company, even a mere sketch, can sometimes be difficult to find, especially if the company is small or of relatively minor importance in its industry. Consider the Web as a source for some of this hard-to-find information. While some history often can be gleaned from even the briefest of company pages–if only a date of establishment and the names of the founders–many companies provide more, sometimes in-depth history at their sites. The Ford Motor Company (*http:/www.ford.com*), for example, offers a lengthy history, illustrated with rare photographs. It is more common to see something briefer, often a section entitled "Milestones," such as provided at the Audi site (*http://www.audi.com*), which takes the form of a list of important dates in the company's history.

Employment Opportunities. Often job-seekers come to the library hoping to find information about job openings and working conditions at particular companies, information which usually is not available in standard resources. Fortunately, larger companies sometimes use their Web presences to attract desirable employees as well as customers. A Web site provides an opportunity for a company to describe career paths and employment benefits, give a sense of its career philosophy, and supply contact information. Because daily updating is possible, specific openings may be listed. The Ford Motor Company's "Career Center," accessible from its Web home page (*http://www.ford.com*), is a model Web package of career information. Examples of other sites which have job and career information include Digital Video (*http://www.c-cube.com/ccube*) and Boeing (*http://www.boeing.com*).

Corporate Profile. Sometimes a quick summary of a company's goals, range of products, size, and customer-base is hard to find and must be assembled from a variety of sources. On the Web, many companies give their own capsule summaries, including the standard information and often interesting items such as competitive and safety records. Competing for notice on the Web, a smaller company is especially likely to articulate its particular emphasis or uniqueness clearly and immediately.

Locations. A list of a company's branch offices, manufacturing facilities, retailers, or dealerships is sometimes difficult to find. Fortunately, companies often provide in their Web sites the means for regional customers to do business easily with them. Northwestern Mutual Life Insurance Company (*http://www.NorthwesternMutual.com*), for example, allows one to browse lists of all its offices and agents, divided by state. Similarly, car companies typically provide information about local dealerships and manufacturers give locations of regional facilities.

Financial. Although financial information on publicly traded corporations is readily available elsewhere, it should be mentioned that many corporations include financial records at their Web site. Some, like American Express (*http://www.AmericanExpress.com*) and Boeing (*http://www.boeing.com*), post their annual reports, including letters to shareholders. The seeker of financial statements should also be aware of the U.S. Securities and Exchange Commission's EDGAR database (*http://www.sec.gov*), which contains reports by most companies required to file forms with the SEC, archived back to 1994.

Communication. It is customary at a company Web site to include a link that allows a visitor to send email to the company. In the interactive spirit of the Web, most companies seem eager to communicate with people who have visited their sites. Even a company as large as Dow Chemical invites immediate contact concerning a product or service. Email access is a boon to library patrons with questions or looking for additional information about a company.

Marketing. Corporate Web sites may be looked upon, in themselves, as examples of how a company portrays itself, advertises its products, targets its buyers, and creates interest. We can observe the company's exploration of the ways to use this very new interactive technology; the marketing lessons are vivid and interesting as new rules are surely being written. Consider how the lines between fun, information, and product promotion blur in Ragu's "Mama's Cucina" [*cucina* is kitchen in Italian] (*http://www.eat.com*), a multi-layered site in which the character of an older Italian woman, Mama, points the way to features like "Mama's Italian Cookbook," "Learn to Speak Italian," "Italian Art & Architecture," and encourages users to email her, warning " . . . and mind your manners." Examples of more traditional uses of visual and sound images, contests, and other means to create or foster interest in products can be found throughout corporate Web sites.

Corporate Image. The information found in a printed directory may express only certain factual aspects of a company. Analyzing a company's Web site, however, will often provide some insight into the image the company wishes to project, particularly to its audience of Net users. In that a Web presence is a company's own promotional tool, using it to communicate strongly its chosen image is likely to be a priority.

The revealed image can be as simple as that found in a logo or a slogan, or can merit more analysis. For example, consider the total effect of Budweiser's home page (*http://www.budweiser.com*), with its college-oriented contests, Usenet-like message exchange board, and educational sections on beer, the environment, and alcohol awareness. The image projected is that of a fun, yet sophisticated company, modern and socially responsible. A more serious image is conveyed by First Chicago Capital Markets,

Inc. (*http://www.fccm.com*), an investment bank, which communicates soundness and security with spare, smart graphics and business-like provision of copious informational text.

Philosophy. A statement of a company's business philosophy, its beliefs or service commitments, often can be found on its home page, sometimes stated as simply as that of A&M Landscaping's, "We have professional experience, offer very reasonable rates, give free estimates, and are dedicated to avoiding the use of harmful chemicals on your lawn" (*http://www.tiac.net/users/adweiss*). Many companies, however, take advantage of the space the Web allows for elaboration. An example is found in the several-page corporate profile posted by Hyperion Software, which details the company's philosophy, vision, applications of products, and service commitment (*http://www.hysoft.com*).

Availability of Information. Sometimes information about a company can be found only on the Web, if one excludes phone and other strictly local directories. As more and more smaller companies and sole proprietorships establish Web presences, the Web becomes an important source of exclusive company information. In this sense, the Web joins with electronic phone and business directories as an important place to look when a sought-for company has fallen through the cracks of the printed directories.

Navigating the vast World Wide Web has become considerably easier with the development of search engines and directories. Nevertheless, using these tools most effectively requires specific knowledge; even then, it is not always easy to zero-in on the sought-after information. The next section will discuss how to use these tools effectively to find company Web sites.

PART TWO: FINDING A COMPANY'S WEB SITE

The most direct way to connect to a company's Web site is to enter the company's Web address, its URL (Universal Resource Locator), in the Location line of your Web browser. If you do not know the URL of the company you are seeking, and it is a very large company, you might make a guess. A large corporation might mount its Web pages on its own computer; its URL might have as its unique parts simply the company's name plus .com. For example, the URL for Boeing is *http://www.boeing.com*

If the above methods do not work or apply, you will need to use a Web finding aid to locate the home page of the company you are seeking. The major aids on the World Wide Web are search engines and directories. Each has advantages and disadvantages when used to search for a company's Web site. The following section will describe recommended WWW search engines and directories and give tips on using them effectively to connect to company Web sites.

Search Engines

Search engines are databases that collect the URLs of Web pages or other Internet resources. When you access a search engine, you are presented with a form onto which you type a text string. The engine retrieves a list of links to Web resources that match the word or phrase you have entered.

An advantage of using a search engine to locate a company is immediacy; if your search is successful, you will retrieve a link that will get you to the company's home page without your having to browse through perhaps several directory trees. However, since search engines comb with varying degrees of discrimination through sometimes thousands of Web URLs in which your term occurs, you may retrieve many links in which your sought-for company is only mentioned peripherally.

With some knowledge of how to use a search engine to its best advantage, you can increase your chances of quickly retrieving a link to a company's home page. Here are some of the most widely-used search engines and tips for using them to find company pages.

Alta Vista

http://altavista.digital.com

This is one of the largest search engines on the Web, claiming a database of 22 million Web pages. If the company you are seeking is small and potentially hard-to-find, choosing a very large search engine is a good strategy.

Alta Vista will accept searches consisting of one or several words, then find documents containing as many of these words as possible, ranked according to the frequency with which these words are found in the first few words of the document (for example, in the title of a Web page). Thus, entering *american greetings* will bring up the link to the company's home page fairly high on the list of hundreds of other entries that include one or another of the words. If your results are not precise enough, try entering the company's name enclosed in quotation marks—*"american greetings"*—guaranteeing that your results will be instances only of those words occurring in adjacency.

If a company's home page is still illusive, consider some other strategies for narrowing your search. First, Alta Vista allows you to choose to search the Web or Usenet; when looking for a company's home page, you should restrict your searching to the Web. Secondly, Alta Vista supports the Boolean operators AND, OR, NOT, NEAR (within 10 words); try searches such as, *"american greetings"* AND home page or *"american greetings"* AND home. Another strategy is to AND the company's name with the phrase *url:home:html*, for example, *"american greetings"* AND *url:home.html*. This clever strategy, suggested in Alta Vista's help page, will bring up sites that have *home.html* in their URLs–not a guarantee that you will find a particular company's home page, but a strategy worth trying. Sometimes including a product name or type of business with the company's name will help eliminate irrelevant items. For example, *the search acme and supermarket* eliminates scores of irrelevant hits had only "acme" been entered.

Lycos

http://www.lycos.com

With access to 10,000,000 Web pages, Lycos is not as extensive as Alta Vista. It is, however, a large and easy-to-use search engine, effective for finding most businesses on the Web.

Lycos supports the Boolean operators AND and OR, with the default being OR. Lycos restricts itself to Web pages and does not support quotation marks. One can improve the precision of a company search by choosing among Lycos' five levels of relevance, "loose match" on one end to "strong match" at the other. The search *american AND greetings*, using the "strong match" option, retrieves the company's home page at the top of the list of results.

Yahoo! Search Page

http://www.yahoo.com/search.html

This engine searches Yahoo!'s index of 80,000 Web sites. With access to a much smaller portion of the Web than Alta Vista or Lycos, Yahoo! might be most effectively chosen when the sought-after company is large or potentially easy to find. This search engine supports Boolean AND and OR. Of the three choices available for restricting searches–Yahoo! Listing, Usenet Newsgroups, or Email Addresses–choose "Yahoo! Listing" when searching for company or other Web pages.

WebCrawler

http://webcrawler.com

This engine defaults to a Boolean OR when more than a single word is entered, but gives higher relevance scores to results that contain all the words, an application of "natural language searching," useful for casual searching when one wishes to cast the widest net possible. For company searching, consider using the Boolean operator NEAR (which allows specifying proximity within a specific number of words) and ADJ (the words next to one another). For example, try searches such as *digital ADJ equipment ADJ corporation* and *acme NEAR4 supermarket.*

Though particular search engines differ, it is possible to summarize the general points and strategies for effective company searching: (1) consider the size of the engine; use the largest engines, like Alta Vista for the smallest or hardest-to-find companies; (2) restrict searches to Web pages when using those engines that include searching of Usenet groups and email addresses; (3) use quotation marks, Boolean operators, and proximity operators when they are available and can be helpful; and (4) include words like "homepage," "home," or words that describe a product or a business to narrow your results to the company's main site.

Directories

Directories organize links to Web sites in hierarchical, topical categories. By choosing a general category, for example, "Business and Economics," and working your way through the subheadings, you can find your desired company links. Searching for a company using a Web directory has some advantages over using a search engine. For one thing, when you locate your company in a directory, the link will most likely take you to the company's main Web site, eliminating the need for you to wade through irrelevant or peripheral links. Secondly, directories allow an opportunity to browse through lists of related companies, facilitating comparison, industry research, business-to-business dealings, or online-shopping. A disadvantage of using a directory to find a company's site is that it can take time to locate the directory, decide the likely subheading path, and find the desired company. Sometimes the company one is seeking is not where one expects to find it, or not in the directory at all. Nevertheless, when one has the time to spend or is fairly certain about where to look, directories provide a good way to get cleanly to a company's home page. What follows is a list of some of the best directories on the Web in which to find company pages.

Yahoo!–Companies

http://www.yahoo.com/Business_and_Economy/Companies/

The popular Yahoo! provides a quick way to reach the home pages of over 10,000 companies. Starting at the Yahoo! Home Page and following the divisions *Business and Economy/Companies*, one will find a list organized by 145 line-of-business categories, leading to links for particular companies. By choosing a slightly different route–*Business and Economy/Companies/Indices*–one will find a list of business categories leading to links for other company directories on the Web. Using Yahoo!–Companies, one can get to the home pages of thousands of companies, commercial services, and individuals in business for themselves.

Industry Net

http://www.industry.net/

This directory of mostly product-oriented companies was designed primarily to help buyers and sellers in the manufacturing sector find each other.

Of interest to the seeker of corporate information are the subsystems *Industry Net Linker*–which provides links to over 6,000 Web sites through over 30 industrial categories–and *Regional Buying Guide*, which compiles custom lists of company links from the user's selection of U.S. regions and industry categories. A search engine is available in both subsystems.

The Web Wanderer's List of Industrial Company Home Pages

http://www.xnet.com/~blatura/industry.shtml/

Like Industry Net, this directory provides access primarily to the manufacturing and process industries and the companies that support them. The directory offers an easy-to-browse list of about 90 companies, public and private, plus links to other company directories on the Web. This is a good place to look for some of the larger manufacturers, like 3M and Boeing, in addition to the home pages of trade associations. A companion site, *The Web Wanderer's List of Computer-Related Company Home Pages* (*http://www.xnet.com/~blatura/computer.shtml*), emphasizes companies and services for personal computers and their users, although pages for some larger systems are found here as well. All the major producers are here, such as IBM, Apple, and Hewlett-Packard, and smaller companies and suppliers of peripherals as well.

Business World

http://www.dks.com/dks/businessworld/

This is another directory that exists primarily to facilitate business-to-business activity, in this case emphasizing global trade. *Business World* serves "companies from around the world who wish to introduce their product(s) and/or service(s) online, via the Internet." In line with this emphasis, the directory provides links to U.S. Government agencies, online shopping, chambers of commerce, and trade associations as well as to both large and small corporations organized under type-of-business categories.

International Net Directory

http://www.pronett.com/

Web pages for hundreds of companies, large and small, in specific countries can be accessed from this directory. The well-designed hierarchical menus begin with regions of the world, then move to individual countries, then business categories.

Biz-Web

http://www.bizweb.com/

A large directory, *Biz-Web* currently provides links to 3,673 companies, ranging from those on the Fortune 500 list to smaller companies that use the Web primarily as a mail order service. One can search by any combination of company name, product words, or service words, or browse through a nicely-detailed hierarchical listing of business categories. Links to companies that accept online orders are identified on the list.

BigBook

http://www.bigbook.com

BigBook has at least two good reasons to recommend it for reference. First is size; it provides name, address, phone, and business category for

11 million U.S. businesses. Second, it provides a street-level map for each business. All of these points of information are searchable. The map searching is particularly nice; a user can focus on a map at national, state, city, or street level and receive a list of businesses located therein. This huge databases exists most practically for reference as a flexible online Yellow Pages. It will not provide access to the official home pages of the larger companies, but it will provide what might be the only available information on the Web for many smaller companies.

Open Market's Commercial Sites Index

http://www.directory.net/

Though not listing anywhere near as many companies as *BigBook*, *Commercial Sites Index* contains a large number of business listings, around 26,000. Its advantage over *BigBook* is that it connects the user to businesses that already have a Web presence, that is, to the established home pages of companies who have submitted their URLs to the Index administrator. Look here for hard-to-find service providers of all kinds—hotels, restaurants, technological services, sports teams, shipping services, and manufacturers, to list a few—from all around the world. Users can search by company name, URL, or keywords, or browse an alphabetical listing.

Investor Relations Resource: Public Companies

http://networth.galt.com

This directory provides an easy way to reach the home pages of 1,471 public corporations found on stock exchanges throughout the world. Users can browse an index of companies divided alphabetically or search for companies by name, ticker symbol, or description.

Job Trak

http://www.jobtrak.com/profiles

Job Trak is unique in the world of Web company directories in that it specifically provides a way for students who are seeking jobs and employers who wish to enlist college graduates to find each other. It claims 600 new jobs posted each day by over 170,000 employers, who can target specific colleges among those whose placement centers participate in the *Job Trak* program. Students can forward their resumes directly to the employers who post job listings. *Job Trak* provides links to company home pages as well, though to a relative few (about 300) through an easy-to-browse list. These are mostly larger corporations of diverse kinds.

CONCLUSION

As the Internet and its popular graphic interface, the World Wide Web, continue rapidly to evolve, the discussion about its place in libraries, particularly reference services, rests necessarily on unsettled ground. Many librarians feel, that the Web will finally serve best as a complement or supplement to, and not as a replacement for, more traditional reference resources.

This article supports that model by describing how the Web can provide company information of a different type than is easily found in more traditional library resources. Specifically, corporate Web sites typically provide information about company history, employment opportunities, regional locations, company philosophy, and corporate news. They may provide in-depth information about products and offer the opportunity of direct communication through email. As companies explore the power of the World Wide Web to advertise and promote their products and services, their pages give us insights into their desired images and marketing strategies. Perhaps most importantly from a practical standpoint, the Web may provide the only readily available information about thousands of companies that are left out of printed, nationally-focused directories.

This article also has described methods for finding corporate sites on the Web, specifically by using WWW search engines and directories. Search engines enable the user to find quickly links to information related to a company, though they may not provide instant access to its home page. Directories provide direct links to corporate home pages, yet they necessitate navigating through hierarchical lists.

REFERENCES

1. "SMT Supplement," *Sales & Marketing Management*, March 1996, 32.
2. Ellsworth, Jill H. "Staking a Claim on the Internet," *Nation's Business*, January 1996, 29-31.

NETWORKING

Building a Better Mousetrap: Networking with Community Business Resources

Linda Medaris
Mark Manley

SUMMARY. Businesses and inventors require timely and complete information relative to the new products they are developing. Requests for business information often require an understanding of an industry that goes beyond the scope of services provided by the library. It is important for the librarian to build linkages to community business resources such as the Small Business Development Center (SBDC), or others whose purpose is to assist local businesses, inventors, and new product developers. Patent and trademark searches and

Linda Medaris is Coordinator of Public Services, Ward Edwards Library, Library 122, Central MO State University, Warrensburg, MO 64093 (E-mail: medaris@cmsuvmb.cmsu.edu). Mark Manley is affiliated with the Center for Technology and Small Business Development, Grinstead Suite 14, Central MO State University, Warrensburg, MO 64093.

[Haworth co-indexing entry note]: "Building a Better Mousetrap: Networking with Community Business Resources." Medaris, Linda, and Mark Manley. Co-published simultaneously in *The Reference Librarian* (The Haworth Press, Inc.) No. 58, 1997, pp. 41-48; and: *Business Reference Services and Sources: How End Users and Librarians Work Together* (ed: Katherine M. Shelfer) The Haworth Press, Inc., 1997, pp. 41-48. Single or multiple copies of this article are available for a fee from The Haworth Document Delivery Service [1-800-342-9678, 9:00 a.m. - 5:00 p.m. (EST). E-mail address: getinfo@haworth.com].

41

other research related to new products present an ideal way for librarians and community business consultants to work together. Such a relationship exists on the campus of Central Missouri State University where library staff and the staff of the SBDC on campus have assisted new product developers by providing patent and trademark searches, and technology and market research. Many clients of this partnership have successfully brought products and services to the marketplace. *[Article copies available for a fee from The Haworth Document Delivery Service: 1-800-342-9678. E-mail address: getinfo@haworth.com]*

INFORMATION NEEDS OF BUSINESSES, NEW PRODUCT DEVELOPERS, INVENTORS, AND MANUFACTURERS

When an inventor or business has developed a new product or invented that better mousetrap, a lot of time and effort should go into planning and refining the product. Often a catchy name is given to the product and the impulse is to rush headlong into patenting or production. Before an inventor spends a significant amount of money, he needs information on legal, technical and marketing issues. Much of the information that the client needs is available in the library through traditional print and electronic resources; however, information alone is not sufficient. There is a need for good problem definition and for information interpretation that is beyond the role of most reference librarians.

The steps a business or inventor should use in researching the information needed to bring that person's product to market can be described as:

PROBLEM DEFINITION→RESEARCH→DATA INTERPRETATION

Normally, the library's role is in the research step of the process. Problem definition and data interpretation are often left to the business client. Reference librarians may encounter poorly defined questions from a business or inventor. Business consultants have seen clients wrestle with too much information or with complex information that they are not able to interpret (i.e., patents or trademark citations).

At Central Missouri State University a partnership involving the Center for Technology and Small Business Development (Center for Technology) and Library Services successfully addresses this challenge. Through this partnership the Center for Technology, whose purpose is to assist businesses and inventors, provides the problem definition through one or more hours of business consultation with a client. The Center brings the problem definition to the librarian and assists in conducting the research step of the process. Finally, after data collection the Center interprets that information and provides a concise report to the client.

HOW THE PARTNERSHIP STARTED

Library Services began its partnership with the Center for Technology in 1988 and at that time Central librarians had several years of experience searching DIALOG databases. However, none of the searchers had experience searching patent and trademark databases. The Dean of Library Services asked the General Reference librarian to assist the Center for Technology in doing some patent searches. One or sometimes two of their engineers came to the library and the *Claims/U.S. Patents Abstracts* database was searched. It appeared that this was to be a "temporary" arrangement since the Center sent their engineers to learn DIALOG searching, and once their computer equipment was installed, it was assumed that they would do their own patent and trademark searches.

Online searching for patents was not that much different from searching a bibliographic database. The engineers described their client's product and a search strategy was constructed using a combination of keywords and patent class numbers. A necessary resource was the *Manual of Classification*, a government publication compiled by the U.S. Department of Commerce Patent and Trademark Office listing the classes and subclasses for patented items.

The Center decided it was more cost effective to have someone using DIALOG on a regular basis to actually do the searching rather than rely on their engineers to keep up with search techniques. This formed the basis for a relationship between Library Services and the Center for Technology that presently continues. Currently the partnership results in about one hundred client-funded searches being conducted annually. A number of past clients have gone on to introduce successful new products to the market.

NEW PRODUCTS AND PATENTS

Before beginning production of a new item, a business or an inventor needs many types of information. Since less than 5 percent of new products that are patented reach the market successfully, a search of the market is not sufficient; a patent search should be conducted. One of the first steps in any new product development process is to have a patent search done to see if there has been a patent granted on a similar item. If the product developer has indeed invented a unique product, he may then want to protect the idea by applying for a patent so others will not copy his idea. With patents it is necessary to get the assistance of someone knowledgeable about patent law to assist in interpreting the search. A patent attorney or agent is usually required and it would be a good idea for the reference librarian to build linkages to these individuals in the community. The librarian might contact the local SBDC or Service Corps of Retired Executives (SCORE) chapter to help build the link as these organizations sometimes have connections already. Finding out if someone has previously used the name that the developer has given to that ideal product is as important as the patent itself. If someone is already calling his/her mouse trap "Mice on Ice," a new developer had better come up with another name for his new mouse trap that freezes mice.

Common Myths Inventors Have About Patents and New Products

Myths	Fact
A letter to myself will establish my date of product conception.	*It won't, participate in the Patent Office Disclosure Document Program to establish date of idea conception.*
My product is so good it will market itself.	*Less than 5% of patented products reach the market successfully. Marketing is the the key to success.*
I will sell just an idea to a large company.	*Most large companies are not interested in your idea. Companies do buy ideas but usually only after the inventor has brought it successfully to the market on a small scale.*
I can file my own patent and save money.	*The process of filing a patent is very unfriendly to the novice. Attempts usually result in a waste of time and money for the inventor.*

A wise product developer does not start producing and marketing his product without determining the answers to these questions. In the event someone already has patented a similar product or has trademarked that name, the developer will likely be hearing from the legal representatives of the patent or trademark holder. *Patent it Yourself* by David Pressman is an excellent reference book on patent law for inventors just getting started. Besides intellectual property (patents, trademarks, and copyrights) a new product developer may wish to research issues like regulations, manufacturing, financing, and marketing the new products. In addition to library resources, the reference librarian will want to have a network of consultants to help the client get a good problem definition.

THE BUSINESS CONSULTANT'S ROLE: DEFINING THE PROBLEM AND ADDING VALUE TO INFORMATION

Has enough thought been given to how "Mice on Ice" will be produced? If it is going to be labor-intensive to produce, the price to the consumer may have to be too high to make it attractive. The average person may not know anything about methods of production, marketing, or financing. The business consultant can assist in defining the problems associated with these issues.

When a consultant works with a client, he needs to thoroughly understand the client's product. Some of the clients have a detailed drawing and written explanation of the product and these generally require a simpler patent search. Other inventors, however, have only sketchy drawings and little or no written description. It is important that the consultant have a thorough understanding of the product for the information gathering phase of the process to be successful.

As a client develops a product, he may ask a general question like: "Is there a market for mouse traps?" Or he may wrongly assume that the product is so good that it will sell itself! The business consultant, after studying the benefits of the product may refine the question to something much more specific like: "What is the market for mouse traps in the hotel industry?" Answering the general question usually gives the client an excess of information he cannot condense. Answering the specific question gives the client information he can use to address a specific market, in this case the hotel industry. Armed with this specific knowledge, the client can make an intelligent decision whether or not to market to the hotel industry.

Once in a while a student or public client comes to the library asking at the Reference Desk for assistance with patent information. Within Library Services a specific librarian has been identified to work with new product development and patent information. If the client is clear about what he needs and seems to understand the patent process, a patent or a trademark search is conducted. The majority of persons, however, have many questions about the patent or trademark search and what happens after the search is accomplished. Many clearly do not understand the patent or trademark process. In these cases questions pertaining to the search are answered and then the client is referred to the Center for Technology for the needed information. Sometimes this results in an engineer from the Center coming back to do a search on that product.

THE LIBRARY'S ROLE: SUPPLYING INFORMATION

There are three ways a patent search can be done. A traditional patent search is done by a searcher in Washington, D.C. working in the Patent Search Room of the U.S. Patent and Trademark Office. The search is typically contracted by a patent attorney and paid for by the client. The traditional search is a thorough one and it is the most expensive. A second option is for the client to conduct his own search at a patent depository library. This search will not be as complete and it will take some time, often twenty to thirty hours, for an inventor starting from scratch with no prior experience. A third option is to conduct a search electronically using an online database like DIALOG or a CD-ROM product. This option provides a good first look for inventors that are just starting out and can often be done for one-third the cost of a traditional search.

At Central the early *Claims/U.S. Patents Abstracts* database searches were done with just a communications program typing in the search as it progressed. As software programs such as *ProSearch* became available, those were utilized for their ability to type in searches off line, to save online time and which also had an accounting function to keep track of clients and fees. *DialogLink for Windows* software is now being used.

At one point Library Services experimented and tried a patent database on CD-ROM. However, it was decided that DIALOG was superior because of the flexibility in searching and the detailed information available.

After the business or inventor initially meets with Center for Technology staff, an appointment is scheduled to conduct appropriate searches. Search sessions can be brief when searching a single patent or trademark or lengthy when information is needed for several clients. Some of the searches are straight-forward and simple, and some searches become quite complex in seeking information for a particularly elusive product. When the search is completed, a copy of the accounting form is printed for library records and a draft copy of the search is printed for the Center. The search is edited, removing the extraneous material such as telecommunications information and database costs, and is printed on a laser printer for the Center to give to the client. This process was developed to satisfy the particular requirements of the Center and its clients.

The Center for Technology uses the draft copy of the search to identify products with similarities. Those patent numbers are noted and a student assistant comes to the library to pull appropriate issues of the *Official Gazette the U.S. Patent Office* from the Government Documents area to make photocopies of the abstract of the appropriate patents. Central's Documents area has copies of the patent *Gazettes* from 1966 and the trademark *Gazettes* from 1971 to the present. The Center also uses MicroPatents Patents Web at *http://www.micropat.com/* to retrieve patent documents.

Document delivery became much simpler with DIALOG's SourceONE which is the favored choice when obtaining copies of the complete patent. Prior to SourceONE, traditional Interlibrary Loan was used to obtain patents from a patent depository such as St. Louis Public Library or Linda Hall Library.

Business Assistance Organizations

Assistance available to business varies from state to state. Places to start.

Small Business Development Center (SBDC)

These centers exist in each state and are set up to provide no-cost consulting services to small business. Most centers exist at colleges and universities although a few are housed in government offices. For the office near call the Association of Small Business Development Centers 703-448-6124.

U.S. Small Business Association (SBA)

Provides a variety of services including loan guarantees. Usually have a Senior Core of Retired Executives (SCORE) to provide some consulting assistance.

State Economic Development

Most states have a State Office of Economic Development to coordinate and provide for business assistance within the state.

Providing the results of a search to your client is a valuable service. The next step is to interpret the information; this "value added" phase should not be left to an untrained client. The reference librarian can expedite the process by building linkages to the experts, such as a business consultant in the community.

OPPORTUNITIES FOR THE LIBRARIAN TO BUILD RELATIONSHIPS WITH THE BUSINESS COMMUNITY

What began as a temporary arrangement for Library Services personnel to perform patent and trademark searches for the Center for Technology and Small Business Development on the campus of Central Missouri State University has grown into a long-term relationship. In order to build relationships, the reference librarian needs to be aware of organizations that assist new product developers and how to network with them. There are associations such as the Chamber of Commerce and local inventor groups. Meetings held by these organizations are usually open to the public and information specialists such as librarians are welcome to attend. In addition to associations, there are professional organizations such as law firms, business, engineering and marketing consultants and custom manufacturers. In general, a novice inventor should work with local organizations. A number of scam businesses prey upon the novice inventor charging a large amount of money for services poorly performed. A number of government-funded business assistance organizations exist. One of the best for start-up companies is the Small Business Development Centers (SBDC). An SBDC program exists in every state. Offices are usually located on university campuses or in local government offices. *The States and Small Business: a Directory of Programs and Activities* is a book which lists the business assistance organizations by state. The Center for Technology and Small Business Development on the campus of Central Missouri State University specializes in working with inventors and would be glad to send additional information on business assistance organizations in your area or information on working with inventors (816-543-4402).

REFERENCES

Official Gazette of the United States Patent and Trademark Office. Washington, D.C.: U.S. Government Printing Office.

Pressman, D. (1995). *Patent it Yourself* (4th ed.). Berkeley, CA, Nolo Press.

U.S. Department of Commerce, Patent and Trademark Office. (1992). *Manual of Classification.* Washington, D.C.: U.S. Government Printing Office.

U.S. Small Business Administration. (1993). *The States and small business: A directory of programs and activities.* Washington, D.C.: U.S. Government Printing Office.

The Information Specialist Customer Partnership

Christine Bennett
Duane Napp

SUMMARY. "To make significant contributions at appropriate points in the research process, information specialists must be positioned for proactive service to their users" (Von Seggern p. 101). At the National Center for Manufacturing Sciences Manufacturing Information Resource Center, information specialists are part of their customer's team and contribute valuable expertise, information, and skills. The synergy of this relationship will be illustrated by describing three projects where these knowledge workers collaborated with their customers. From this experience, these information professionals share recommendations for fostering the customer librarian partnership. In conclusion, the synergistic practices described are related to literature on the topic of librarian customer teamwork. *[Article copies available for a fee from The Haworth Document Delivery Service: 1-800-342-9678. E-mail address: getinfo@haworth.com]*

Information specialists at The National Center for Manufacturing Sciences (NCMS) Manufacturing Information Resource Center (MIRC) deliver information services in two ways. One is more traditional and episodic where library services are provided to the patron's questions by information professionals residing in an information center. The second

Christine Bennett is Information Specialist, and Duane Napp is Project Manager, Lead Free Solder Project, The National Center for Manufacturing Sciences, 3025 Boardwalk, Ann Arbor, MI 48108.

[Haworth co-indexing entry note]: "The Information Specialist Customer Partnership." Bennett, Christine, and Duane Napp. Co-published simultaneously in *The Reference Librarian* (The Haworth Press, Inc.) No. 58, 1997, pp. 49-57; and: *Business Reference Services and Sources: How End Users and Librarians Work Together* (ed: Katherine M. Shelfer) The Haworth Press, Inc., 1997, pp. 49-57. Single or multiple copies of this article are available for a fee from The Haworth Document Delivery Service [1-800-342-9678, 9:00 a.m. - 5:00 p.m. (EST). E-mail address: getinfo@haworth.com].

way on a regular basis is as a member of a project team where the specialist attends team meetings, becomes an "expert" on the subject of the team's project, serves as the project's information consultant and participates in developing one of the team's end products or deliverables. This information specialist/customer teamwork differs from the episodic information provision of information in several ways. It:

- is a synergistic, ongoing, interactive relationship between the information specialist and customers who are a team
- involves the librarian becoming an "expert" on that field to provide the information needs of that project on a continuing basis until it is complete
- includes the gathering of information and its analysis and presentation for the purpose of educating the project team
- is a proactive approach where the information specialist is conveniently in the customer's environment rather than in his or her stationery location
- facilitates the role of the information specialist as consultant who is immediately available to solve information based project issues
- brings additional financial resources to supplement the information center budget since the information center is reimbursed for the information professional's services

The following three examples illustrate this type provision of information on a regular basis as part of a team. Each example provides details about the librarian/customer partnership and describes the team's end product. Recommendations about fostering this collaborative approach to meeting the customer's needs follow. In conclusion, the practices identified in this article are compared to literature on customer/librarian teamwork.

WHEN THE TEAM NEEDS A SCOUT AND AUTHOR

At the request of Duane Napp, Project Manager for the Lead Free Solder Project, the information professional's role evolved from a traditional one of providing information upon request to one of being a watchdog and researching lead legislation and regulation and presenting the findings at quarterly Lead Free Solder Project Team meetings. This team is comprised of technologists located throughout the United States involved in this over $8 million research project. Participants are from AT&T, the Navy Electronics Manufacturing Productivity Facility, Ford, GM-Hughes

Division, GM-Delco Electronics, MicroFab Technologies, the National Institute of Standards and Technology, Rensselaer Polytechnic Institute, Rockwell International, Sandia National Laboratories, Texas Instruments, and Hamilton Standard Division of United Technologies Corporation.

Mr. Napp's experience in academia influenced his belief in the importance of regular use of information by these researchers. He invited the librarian to present at the quarterly meeting to facilitate greater usage of library resources by the team. This presentation raised some important issues regarding the impact that legislation and regulation might have on the interconnect industry and the team decided to prepare a white paper to describe the project and goals. The focus of the paper would be "to communicate the electronics industry's perspective on the issue of lead use to everyone who is concerned about it" (*Lead and the Electronics Industry*, p. 1).

The information professional, nominated by the team to the white paper committee, wrote the section on lead legislation, lead usage, and the status of the electronics industry. Additional information responsibilities including providing literature searches on patents, toxicology, and economics and selecting related materials for the collection.

THE TEAM NEEDS TO KNOW
BEST PRACTICES FOR AN INFLUENTIAL REPORT

In the second example of the information specialist customer partnership, Marti Reesman, Project Manager for the Developing Manufacturing Trade Academies Study, added an information specialist to her team which consists of the following NCMS employees: a technical writer, a library manager, an information specialist, a contracts specialist, and an administrative assistant.

The information specialist's responsibilities for this project include "researching and preparing a report on the school-to-work efforts being conducted in other states, current school-to-work efforts within traditional school settings, information about labor force requirements and skill development, and methods of communication/marketing to manufacturing firms." In addition, the information professional will do site visits to observe and survey academy administrators and participating employers.

The end product of all the efforts of the team participants is a "report that will include a summary of the academy visits, research findings, and survey results, with analysis and recommendations. From this information NCMS will develop a technical assistance plan appropriate for statewide implementation" (*Trade Academies: Educational Building Blocks for Tomorrow's Manufacturing Workforce*).

THE INFORMATION SPECIALISTS
EXPAND THEIR KNOWLEDGE AND THE COLLECTION

In the third example of a partnership, a customer [David Sordi, Senior Project Engineer with The Torrington Company] co-authored a book review with the information professional. During a presentation about MIRC capabilities, the information professional discussed MEASURING CORPORATE ENVIRONMENTAL PERFORMANCE to emphasize that reading and reviewing books is an activity that expands our collection and knowledge. As a result of the presentation, David Sordi offered to co-author a review. This illustrates these specialists' receptivity to customer collaboration.

To encourage collaboration, all information specialists in MIRC chose project management subject areas and offered information services to the project teams doing research in these areas. Projects at NCMS involve electronics, environmentally conscious manufacturing, management practices, computer integrated operations, and production equipment and systems. Due to the sheer number of projects, information professionals provide mostly episodic information services and regular services by special arrangements.

FOSTERING THE INFORMATION
SPECIALIST CUSTOMER PARTNERSHIP

What elements are necessary to promote this intensive information specialist customer teamwork?

1. The manager of the information center or library must believe in this approach and support staff participation in it. The professional staff at MIRC decided to participate as information consultants on project teams. The manager fully supported this initiative and consulted with project managers to prepare the way for this partnership with them.
2. The information specialist needs to target a champion or gatekeeper on the project team. Because of his research roots in academia and his role as project team manager, Duane Napp is a gatekeeper or champion for the Lead Free Solder Project. He asks the librarian to do pre-

sentations for his team and refers team members to her. Marti Reesman is a champion of the Michigan Manufacturing Trade Academies
Study partnership. She includes the information specialist in planning
and steering committee meetings, schedules her for presentations and
has asked her to prepare an analysis of the literature on this topic.

3. The information specialist must be able to set priorities and manage
   time. A work day involves traditional episodic library services such
   as "Please run a patent search on xyz," "What does ISO 9002 cover?" or "Rush the following publications" to researching future labor force requirements in manufacturing or writing a report. These
   must be incorporated into a schedule that includes customer requests
   for information, project meetings, updating search skills, departmental and collection development meetings, or attendance and assistance with special committees assignments.

4. The information specialist draws upon his or her skills to complement
   the team. The skills required as part of the partnerships mentioned in
   this paper include writing, presentation charisma, background in behavioral sciences and education, critical thinking, reference, research,
   and organization. The information specialist asked questions, made
   suggestions, participated in conference calls. This insured a high
   quality white paper that met the team's expectations.

5. The information specialist must nurture the customer relationship.
   The setting for a strong librarian customer partnership occurred in
   the Six Sigma Surface Mount Technology Project. Upon the suggestion of the industry champion, the information specialist traveled to
   Digital Equipment Corporation in Ottawa, Ontario with the specific
   assignment of kicking off the project meeting with a brief description of the benefits of using MIRC. The assignment included listen-
   ing carefully to the team participants' presentations and identifying
   ways MIRC information services could help with the project. At the
   end of the meeting, the librarian showed this team how a DIALOG
   search could help them with their project. DIALOG search examples used topics identified during the meeting.

Techniques for keeping the contributions of the information professional active in the minds of the team include contact with both the industry
champion and project manager to discuss further information services
assistance, attending team meetings, and delivery electronic updates.

6. The information specialist must be able to use appropriate resources
   to efficiently locate answers for questions posed by team members.
   The Michigan Manufacturing Trade Academies Study requires that

a literature search and its analysis be done quickly because the entire project must be completed in six months. Therefore, it is imperative that pertinent material be available quickly. This specialist used a school-to-work Internet site, a specialized lending library at Michigan State University and interlibrary loan. In this case, there is no need to own the material and borrowing or obtaining the material electronically is quicker than purchasing it.

7. The information specialist can bring value to the team without having a degree in the field because more than subject expertise is involved. Excellent customer service results when the librarian (1) works with the customers to understand their expectations, (2) is aware that information gathering can cause anxiety for patrons, and (3) establishes open communication to achieve a common goal. These are factors that can influence acceptance by the team.

Neway (p. 140) states that "subject orientation is necessary if the information specialist is to be regarded as a colleague in the research team and provide a high-class information service to maintain this respect." This contrasts with Huston who describes the success of her colleague who dealt with "the literature of women's studies, a field in which he was not formally trained but was self-educated" (p. 77). In the hard sciences, it may be necessary to have a degree to gain the team's respect, but in the soft sciences, as in Parson's case and with the Trade Academies Study, self-education worked. Depending upon the nature of the team's end product, a librarian can be accepted on the team if she/he learns about the subject while providing information needed by the team. For example, with The Lead Free Solder Project, the librarian researched the legislative, regulatory, and economic aspects of the electronics industry and combined this with the technical knowledge of a project member to prepare a paper.

8. The information specialist can persuade management of the value of the information center's contribution because the information specialist has evidence of his/her contribution to the organization. The specialist sees the results of information provision and is part of producing a tangible product. Outsourcing and downsizing are key issues: Information professionals who can demonstrate their contribution to the organization's goals have evidence of their value and advocates in satisfied customers. The librarian becomes an integral part of the fabric that is the company. At NCMS, the information professional worked as a team member to be part of a project whose goal is to be environmentally proactive to implement lead-free alloys in electronics manufacturing operations. She also worked on a

team which assisted the State of Michigan to devise a methodology and tools for working with Michigan's manufacturing firms to build support for and develop manufacturing-focused trade academies for high school students.

RECOMMENDATIONS FROM THE LITERATURE ON LIBRARIAN TEAM PARTICIPATION

These examples are largely anecdotal rather than qualitative. This paper evolved based upon experiences of the information professionals working with project teams. However, it was gratifying to discover that the methods that evolved in the course of these projects are cited in the literature as model ones.

"Although the information specialist should be highly visible and easy to use by all members of the research team, it is often expedient to concentrate information activities on the group's gatekeeper" (Neway, p. 144). She continues by saying gatekeepers have the following characteristics:

- act as the information focal point within the group
- tend to have more interpersonal contacts than their co-workers
- contact more information resources on a regular basis
- use a greater diversity of internal and external sources
- are older, more educated and have a higher status in their organization than their colleagues.

Librarians need to work with gatekeepers to (1) direct information to them because they will more readily disseminate it to the group and (2) gain acceptance by the group. Neway believes that the acceptability of the information specialist as a team member depends how she/he is perceived and used by the gatekeeper (p. 145). At NCMS, Duane Napp and Marti Reesman are the gatekeepers. They are project managers who are the focal point of their respective teams. They are experts in the project's specialty and hold high status in their organizations. They took the initiative to ask the information specialist to participate on their teams and continue to include her in project meetings. If these champions do not exist, they must be recruited.

One of the ways librarians demonstrate their team partnership actions is to "develop tools and techniques to keep the readers continuously informed of the developments in their respective areas of research" (Neway p. 143). For the Lead Free Solder Project, this information specialist monitors legislative and regulatory issues. To quickly browse through current issues of newsletters and journals in subjects related to the projects we have "adopted" is part of our information specialist duties.

Another way that information specialists can show their interest in a team partnership is to maintain contact with each research worker with a view to understanding and keeping up with their respective specific document and information requirements (Neway p. 143). In the NCMS Trade Academies Study, the contracts member has requested a copy of all laws pertaining to minors and work. The Project Manager often stops by to obtain more reading material on school-to-work issues. This information intensive project means active involvement for the team librarian.

An information specialist acts with "professional responsibility to provide inputs that will lead to successful planning, problem solving, and decision making, since [she or he has] a direct share in the quality of the end-products of the research group served" (Neway p. 141). In the Lead Free Solder Project, the librarian contributed one of the deliverables of the project, a white paper. To reach consensus on the final copy of the paper involved many drafts of the paper and a conference call to obtain the project team's approval of the paper. In the Michigan Manufacturing Trade Academies Study, the information specialist prepared an analysis of the literature for the final report. In both projects, the information specialist had a direct involvement and responsibility for the end product.

"Ensure the information provided to each reader is presented in a manner that makes its absorption and utilization convenient with the least waste of time and effort" (Neway p. 143). The project manager for the Six Sigma Surface Mount Technology Project wants all the material he receives to be electronic so that he can distribute it quickly to his project teams members who are widely disbursed. For the Academies Project, the librarian provided electronic notes to the project team.

To promote the information specialist customer partnership requires "provision for accessibility to required documents within reasonable limits of economy" (Neway p. 143). For the Trade Academies study, this specialist used the School-to-Work Internet site, OCLC interlibrary loans and the Michigan Center for Career and Technical Education at Michigan State University to obtain materials quickly at little or no cost.

The information specialist's participation as part of a team is a synergistic, challenging, rewarding, growth experience. It is intense because the specialist, in addition to providing relevant information efficiently, must master a subject, produce an end product, and manage a complex customer relationship as well as deliver information to episodic requests. The participation on a team serves as a mirror for information professionals. They see the results of their searching and research skills form the patron's perspective. Their communication, research, and reference interviewing skills are reflected by the team as feedback, acceptance, and more research. Information specialists from the image reflected due to this experience can accept what worked and change what didn't to benefit future customers.

AUTHOR NOTE

In July 1996, Christine Bennett marked her fourth year as an Information Specialist at NCMS. Her primary function is to provide research services to internal and external customers. Her previous experience includes more than 10 years of operating the library of a high technology R&D firm. Her educational background includes a MILS from The University of Michigan, and a Masters in Counseling and Behavioral Sciences from The University of Wisconsin. She serves on the Michigan Chapter of the Special Libraries Association Strategic Planning Committee and is an active member of Society of Competitive Intelligence Professionals.

Duane Napp is Project Manager at NCMS where he is responsible for environmental conscious manufacturing and electronic packaging technology projects. He has a Ph.D. from University of Minnesota in Electroanalytical Chemistry and 8 years of Academia at Slippery Rock State University and the University of Minnesota. He has 20 years of industrial technical management experience at IBM, Endicott, NY and Austin, TX in packaging technologies of chips, Printed Wiring Boards, Assemblies, Cabling, Connectors, Reliability, Materials and Processes.

REFERENCES

Huston, Mary M. and Willie Parson. "A Model of Librarianship for Combined Learning and Teaching," *Research Strategies*, Vol. 3 No. 2 pp. 75-80.

National Center for Manufacturing Sciences, *Lead and the Electronics Industry: A Proactive Approach*, May, 1995.

National Center for Manufacturing Sciences, *Trade Academies: Educational Building Blocks for Tomorrow's Manufacturing Workforce*, n.d.

Neway, Julie. *Information Specialist as a Team Player in the Research Process*, Greenwood Press, Westport, Connecticut, 1985.

Von Seggern, Marilyn. "Scientists, Information Seeking, and Reference Services," *The Reference Librarian*, no/49-50, 1995.

Information Seeking Behavior
of Business Students:
A Research Study

Joseph D. Atkinson III
Miguel Figueroa

SUMMARY. This study investigates library use and research behavior of business students at California State University San Marcos. A sample of 68 graduate and 91 undergraduate students were surveyed and observed for their behavior in three conceptual domains: query formulation and task assignments, pre-reference process expectations, and post-reference process responses.
Participant observations confirmed many of the student attitudes revealed in the survey. Even with changes in provision of resources in new high tech libraries, findings confirm assumptions of business students' behavior in the earlier literature. *[Article copies available for a fee from The Haworth Document Delivery Service: 1-800-342-9678. E-mail address: getinfo@haworth.com]*

Providing access to business resources in an academic environment is only half the reference process picture. Understanding how business students use the library and identifying the determinants of information seeking behavior of business students completes the reference process picture. Observation research studies have been conducted to determine the

Joseph D. Atkinson III is Business Librarian (Principal Investigator), Library and Information Services, California State University San Marcos, San Marcos, CA 92096. Miguel Figueroa is an MBA student.

[Haworth co-indexing entry note]: "Information Seeking Behavior of Business Students: A Research Study." Atkinson, Joseph D. III, and Miguel Figueroa. Co-published simultaneously in *The Reference Librarian* (The Haworth Press, Inc.) No. 58, 1997, pp. 59-73; and: *Business Reference Services and Sources: How End Users and Librarians Work Together* (ed: Katherine M. Shelfer) The Haworth Press, Inc., 1997, pp. 59-73. Single or multiple copies of this article are available for a fee from The Haworth Document Delivery Service [1-800-342-9678, 9:00 a.m. - 5:00 p.m. (EST). E-mail address: getinfo@haworth.com].

information-seeking behavior of users in various disciplines ranging from historians to scientists, but few studies identify the norms of behavior among business students in an academic environment. Rapid changes in information provision, computerized access, digitized formats in full text, and the plethora of resources on the Internet cause us to reexamine issues of user behavior. We should ask ourselves if these changes in an academic environment have resulted in significant changes in user behavior.

In this study, a survey was conducted to identify user perceptions in a contemporary high technology academic library. The survey sample consisted of undergraduate and graduate students at California State University San Marcos (CSUSM), a new institution with 3,100 students and a significant investment in computerized resources and electronic access. As a control to the sample, a participant observation study was conducted at California State University Dominguez Hills (CSUDH), a larger institution with over 10,000 students. Both schools offer reference research consultation and extensive bibliographic instruction opportunities for business students.

RELATED LITERATURE

Six years ago, LittleJohn and Benson-Talley surveyed California State University Long Beach business faculty and students to determine students' attitudes, perceptions of library use and skills (LittleJohn and Benson-Talley, 1990). Their findings revealed a high use of the library by students when imposed by the faculty or by class assignments. In a model analyzing the problems related to providing reference to users who were executing an imposed assignment, Gross (1995) defined the imposed query *as a request or question that is given to someone else to transact or resolve*. Gross noted that reference librarians found it difficult to clarify or negotiate the query back to the point of origin.

Hawes (1994) wrote an opinion piece in which he called attention to the ever-growing demand and need for increased literacy and skills among business students. Hawes cited Boyer's (Boyer, 1987, pp. 160-162) surprising assessment: (1) A majority of undergraduates spend no more than 2 hours per week in the library; (2) A majority of undergraduates occasionally or never use indexes or look for further references cited in the texts. Hawes used these findings to promote library instruction in the college curriculum. A study by Jones, Drapeau and Godkin (1987) noted that library assignments which were incorporated in the curriculum yielded a positive impact on students' use of the library and development of skills.

The literature reflects other problems reference librarians encounter with students' skills and behavior. LittleJohn and Benson-Talley confirmed findings of earlier studies by Lee and Read (1972) that students lacked the knowledge and skills necessary to make effective use of the library, and used the library primarily as a result of imposition of assignments by faculty.

The Principle of Least Effort which was introduced by Zipf (1949) has applicability in studying library user behavior. The principle states that most researchers tend to choose easily available information sources, even when these resources are objectively of low quality. Researchers will tend to prefer resources that can be found easily rather than higher-quality sources whose use would require a greater expenditure of effort. Mann (1993) provided extensive documentation to validate Zipf's principle, and noted that the principle is not a model in and of itself, but is implied in many information seeking behavior models.

Haythornthwaite (1990) and Baker (1991) provided an assessment of user impatience and inconvenience, and attempted to identify variables which had an impact on user behavior. Exploring the same vein, Lavin (1987) combined a discussion on the value of information with an exploration of users' potential impatience resulting from complexities of business queries, which required significant subject knowledge and bibliographic expertise.

Smyth (1985) and Auster and Choo (1991, 1993) linked user behavior to availability of resources, and discussed user utility of information resources. Specifically, Smyth examined the time value of resources, and Auster and Choo examined preferences for information resources. Auster and Choo's survey indicates that while CEOs receive information from multiple sources, they rely on personal sources for decision-making, and use impersonal sources such as printed resources for awareness of trends in the environment.

Propositions

Propositions are useful in that they are not hypothetical statements in the traditional sense (defining acceptance or rejection of the null), but are operational definitions that provide new insight, and eventually will translate into hypotheses.

Several propositions were gleaned from a review of the literature. These were grouped into domains, all of equal weight in importance:

- Business students prefer electronic resources over print (utility of resources)
- Business students exhibit traits of urgency in their need for business information (impatience and inconvenience)

- Business students spend less than 2 hours per week in the library (impatience and inconvenience)
- Business students infrequently use indexes or citations to further their research (utility of resources)
- Business students have a shorter break-even time allocation if the query is imposed in the form of an assignment than if they were searching for personal gratification (imposed task)
- Business students have an internal break-even concept, and have a utility of immediacy which guides their information seeking behavior (imposed task)

These same propositions were used as a foundation for the areas of examination in the observation study.

Methodology

The research effort was divided into two parts: (1) a survey to identify students' perceptions, and (2) observations by a librarian if the student perceptions were accurate. This study synthesizes relevant propositions that arose in the limited available literature on business students' information-seeking behavior. These propositions formed the basis for the survey questions.

Students were surveyed for their attitudes and perceptions in Fall Semester 1995 and Winter Intercession 1996. The survey was conducted at California State University San Marcos (CSUSM), one of the newer campuses in the California State System, one that contains a technologically up-to-date library. A brief participant observation study was conducted at CSUSM and California State University Dominguez Hills (CSUDH) for comparison of samples and controls, and to confirm the findings in student surveys at CSUSM.

The Sample. The survey sampled 68 of 90 enrolled graduate students, and 91 of 744 enrolled undergraduate students (primarily juniors and seniors). The combined sample size is 159, representing 19 percent of the business students at CSUSM. Inference to other student populations must take into account traditions and paradigms of information access on their respective campuses.

A diary was kept on three students each at CSUSM and CSUDH for the participant observations to confirm the survey findings.

Student Survey Strategy. Survey questions examined student perceptions or preferences to gain awareness of overall trends and preferences. A short questionnaire was distributed before information literacy classes were taught, to avoid prejudicing their findings with additional skills learned.

All students signed a statement indicating that their responses are held in confidentiality, and recognizing that they are the subjects of study. The survey consisted of ten questions asking the students if they were more inclined or less inclined to behave a certain way based on a proposition. The follow-up open-ended question "why" was asked on most of the questions to gain additional insight into the rationale behind their attitudes. The surveys do not allow us to observe actual behavior, but they do provide a window on student attitudes and preferences.

Participant Observation Strategy. The observation research was included as an essential component for validating professional assumptions regarding the reality of student perceptions. Understanding the context of outcomes of behavior is as important as understanding the impact of the setting, and professional librarians are presumed to be familiar with the elements of successful behavior within that setting. The goal is to generate categories, themes or patterns in the "small world" of the business student in an academic environment. All descriptions were checked for face validity, criterion validity and concept validity.

The setting is critical to any observation research assessment, given that it provides a frame of reference for the respondents to be observed and to react and report their beliefs in the survey. CSUSM and CSUDH comparisons offered different settings which might impact the outcomes of behavior. At both locations, students were informed of their status as subjects of observation and that confidentiality would be maintained.

Gaining a true picture of a business student's information-seeking behavior requires study within the frame of library reference services, so participant observation was deemed the most effective method of obtaining that picture. A journal of interactions was maintained, with most of the behavior described in notes as the observation. Student biases, problems, misconceptions, reactions and behaviors were recorded in field notes, and recaptured and fleshed-out in written summaries of reflections and observations.

One of the difficulties of conducting observation studies is employing appropriate terminology to consistently describe influences and outcomes of behavior. The participant observer created profiles and operational definitions from which to draw descriptive classifications. Observations were made using field notes, with accompanying theory notes and method notes added for perspective.

SURVEY FINDINGS

A majority of respondents (100 respondents, 62.7% with a confidence interval of ± 10%) indicated a preference for electronic resources. Two major reasons surfaced as links to the preferences to electronic resources: (1) "faster/easier/quicker/convenient" was the reason for 77 respondents (48.4%) and (2) "familiarity" with electronic resources was the reason for 36 respondents (22.6%). The balance gave no response.

Reason for Preference for Electronic Resources

Reason stated	Responses *n* = 159	Percent of Total
faster/easier/quicker/convenient	77 responses	48.4%
familiarity	36 responses	22.6%
no response	46 responses	29.0%
Total	159	100.0%

Business students infrequently use indexes or citations to further their research. The survey asked the students to check the resources with which they were most familiar, identified by their popular titles or acronyms. Three groups of resources were identified in the survey: (1) Internet-based resources, (2) print-resources, and (3) online services and electronic indexes. Undergraduates and graduate students cited an average of 3 Internet-based resources, choosing among Gopher, Netscape, WWW, Listservs, BB's FTP, Telnet, Internet and Email. They cited print-based resources at a much lower frequency, with undergraduates citing print on average less than once per survey, and graduates at least once per survey. The print-based resources cited were SIC codes, *S&P, Value Line,* and *Moody's.* The online services and indexes were cited by undergraduates and graduate students an average of 3 times, identifying resources such as Public Access Catalogs, CD-ROMs, Dow Jones, ABI/Inform, and LEXIS-NEXIS.

In an effort to gain a clearer view of the students' intentions, we asked the students to respond if they predetermined *how long* they wanted to stay in the library. We expected business students to have predetermined *how long* they wanted to stay in the library, though only a minority responded positively.

A follow-up question to predetermining *how long* was predetermining *how much* was enough information. A minority of CSUSM business students (32.3%) responded that they had predetermined *how much* information was enough. As an extension to this question, the students were queried on *when* they knew when "enough information is enough." They responded in one of two areas: (1) internally directed responses "feeling/

instinctive/intuitive" (60 responses, 38%), or (2) externally directed responses "imposed/assigned/time oriented" (72 responses, 45%). Though their responses indicated that they were either internally or externally directed, they clearly stated that they had developed pre-reference process expectations by making predeterminations of *how much* and *when* enough information was enough.

Paralleling Boyer's assessment of the limited amount of time students spend in the library, 96 (60.4%) CSUSM business students stated they spend 2 hours or less per week in the library, studying or using library resources. The undergraduate students reported a greater number of hours per week overall than graduate students.

Hours per Week Spent in the Library

	0-1 hrs.	2-3 hrs.	4-5 hrs.	6-7 hrs.	8-9 hrs.	10+ hrs.
Undergraduates $n = 76$	21	23	17	5	3	7
Graduates $n = 59$	37	14	6	0	1	1

Extending the question of *how long* they spend in the library, a follow-up question examined their traits of urgency. The student's preference for their relatively short time allocated to use the library draws a portrait of urgency. A majority of the responses (66.5%) expressed a preference to leave the library when they have found what they need.

On the other hand, some behaviors simply require consumption of time, such as browsing. Browsing is a skill and a traditional search function refined in other disciplines, but one might assume that such a time-consuming effort among business students would be conducted only if imposed. The majority (68%) are browsing to satisfy an external need. A summary of the reasons "why" revealed that the users browse primarily for class assignments, lending further credence to the expectation that imposition of assignments in an academic environment is an important determinant of information-seeking behavior.

Seeking to understand student perceptions of their own behavior in response to an imposed assignment or query, students were asked if they would use the library if *required by the instructor*. The vast majority of responses (90%) stated that they were more inclined to use the library when *required by the instructor*. Of course, the significance of this response is presumed to be due in part to the traditions of the academic environment, in which positive student behavior, in this case, use of the library, is a direct reaction to imposition of the assignment by the instructor. An alternate question was included to confirm student perceptions in the previous question by asking if they are more inclined to use the library for their *own interests*. A minority CSUSM business students, 42.5% with a confidence interval of ± 7%, stated that they are more inclined to use the library for their internal self-directed needs.

OBSERVATIONS

Observations were conducted at CSUDH (Dominguez Hills) and CSUSM over three days in Spring Semester 1996, involving a sample of six business students. Here are some of the major observations:

- The students arrived in the library prepared to conduct research, generally with assignment in hand, though at times their problem statement needed refining when the reference negotiation process began.
- Business students preferred to work in groups in the library, and tend to use team-based information-seeking strategies prior to seeking professional assistance of the librarian. They tended to ask reference-type questions of fellow students first, considering the strength of their own network.
- Observed group work was a function of assignments by faculty and the CSUSM mission encouraging working in groups. Delegation of tasks within groups occurred prior to seeking the professional assistance of a librarian.
- Business students sought immediate trade-offs in their allocation of time versus the amount of relevant information retrieved. In addition, they tended to commodify information, treating it as a commodity with an assigned value which has perceived benefits.
- Often, online browsing on public access catalog (PACs) or full-text retrieval systems was minimal, resulting in the students' capturing only the first few screens instead of determining the depth and complexity of the database prior to exiting the search. Once pertinent resources were identified from the retrieved search, the most current was examined, retrieved, copied and/or cited. It should be noted that CSUSM business students use LEXIS-NEXIS heavily, which reveals the most current contents of a search first in its display logic.
- Business students tended to abruptly leave the library in the middle of a search if their predetermined time allocation was depleted. Busy

student schedules resulted in stringent prioritizing, which forced them to parse their time in conjunction with effort expended.

*   Undergraduate business students were surprised to locate "answers" in print resources just as fast as or faster than using electronic resources. "Wired" business students tended to rely on their common sense in locating answers, sometimes incorrectly assuming electronics retrieval was faster than print.
*   Library skills training provided an opportunity to alter a student's choice of tools and improve decisions that balance their use of time and resources. A lack of training results in the student's search being driven by the initial question, rather than availability of a variety of resources. Tools such as pathfinders and subject bibliographies are helpful in locating print resources that provide suggestions.
*   In the academic environment, there is a push (encouragement by faculty and availability of resources) and a pull (time and cost constraints) at work and students' preferences are shaped by these relationships.

IMPLICATIONS FOR REFERENCE LIBRARIANS

The implications of this study for reference librarians are examined within the context of three areas of the reference process: Query formulation and task assignment, pre-reference process expectations, and post-reference process responses. Some of the following implications may call for remolding of the reference process for business students, while other implications confirm conventional wisdom.

QUERY FORMULATION AND TASK ASSIGNMENT

In an academic environment, the imposed query primarily takes the form of a class assignment. The imposition of information seeking by the faculty creates a direct impact on the student's motivation to use the library. As Littlejohn and Benson-Talley found six years ago (1990), the overwhelming majority of students use the library as a place either to study or to complete assignments imposed by the faculty. While assignments are a motivating factor along with the potential of earning good grades, students still exhibit tradeoffs–for example, they may plan to find just enough information to get what they believe will result in a good grade. Rather than planning an optimized search during the query formulation stage, "satisficing" occurs. Satisficing is described in the literature as user behavior that moderates goals and limits search behavior despite the potential of finding better resources (Zipf, 1949, and Simon, 1956).

When assembling the findings on *when* did they know that "enough was enough," the students' responses to this opened-query revealed two distinct clusters. The first cluster of respondents were internally motivated or inward directed, describing knowledge of when enough was enough as "instinct" or "intuition." The second cluster of respondents were externally motivated or outward directed, describing knowledge of when enough was enough as "imposed by instructor," "assigned," or resulting from "time limitations." This second cluster highlights a problem identified in Gross' model, which notes the difficulty reference librarians have when trying clarify an imposed query with someone who may not have a clear idea of the originator's request. The transfer process can result in a less than satisfactory response, unless the originator's goal is to encourage the student to learn the process.

If the findings in this study are true, then we are justified in our belief that imposition of tasks on business students by faculty has a direct impact on their motivation and search behavior.

PRE-REFERENCE PROCESS EXPECTATIONS

Once the user query is defined, the business student begins to develop pre-reference process expectations. While the student may have some expectations prior to a query being developed, this is usually a self-view, world-view, or previous experience with the library. Asking students if they predetermined or planned their quantity of time or their quantity of retrieved information is the first step in identifying variables of expectations that can be clearly tracked, appropriated, and defined. Predetermined expectations which match retrieval within certain need-scale constraints should yield satisfaction. However, predetermining the use of resources is not the same as actually executing behavior. Therefore, the follow-up question asking how many hours they actually spent in the library provides a basis of comparison between what the user predetermines and what the user actually uses.

Predetermining various expectations requires the user to set up a decision path prior to conducting the reference process. The critical decision path influencing business students' choice of resources includes consideration of need-scale constraints such as costs, time and value of money, and opportunity costs (such as thinking time equals money). Perceived potential costs can influence how students realize the value of their time invested in completing a class paper or project; therefore, they may try to find the most efficient way to access information. According to their frame of reference, time is an important constraint, in that it is consumed, and is expended in fixed intervals. On the other hand, money can be expended in varying amounts (for items such as copying, purchasing disks and paying fees). These concepts link together in a scale that identifies incremental increases in expenditures of cost, time, effort, or pleasure providing marginal returns invested—in other words, an internal break-even or optimization scheme.

Given future careers guided by capitalism, profit and efficiency, these students tend to think competitively about their preparation and expenditures, time spent learning and using resources. Observed student behavior consistently demonstrates a preference for electronic resources over print resources. One factor may be the perceived ease of availability of information at a dispensing computer terminal. An underlying factor behind this perception is the students' recognition of time constraints and the value of the information retrieved. For example, a student can access information on full-text systems or CD-ROMs that can be downloaded to a diskette. Editing and review can be accomplished at a less time-consuming pace on a personal computer at home. Therefore, business students, who are predisposed to thinking in terms of time efficiency and cost-effectiveness, make choices reflective of their predisposition.

Further indications of pre-reference process expectations involve encouraging business students to stay current with the latest technology. At CSUSM, hardware and software are regularly updated campus-wide, as a matter of policy. Furthermore, business students infrequently use paper indexes or citations to further their research, viewing this resource as traditional and sometimes cumbersome. In contrast, students may choose an electronic resource, perceiving it to be a more appropriate tool (in addition to its perceived cost-effectiveness), in that it also helps them achieve their goal of staying current with the latest technology. These "environmental" reasons work together to influence student preferences for electronic resources, resulting in a perceived greater utility than print or other resources.

One important qualification to these findings is that a significant minority of older graduate students still perceive print to be a better resource, but this may be due to a lack of familiarity and skills using computer resources.

Group work dramatically demonstrates pre-process expectations in the way students execute research tasks to achieve their research. At CSUSM and CSUDH, students are required to work individually and in groups as a part of their class assignments. When groups are formed for a specific project, specific tasks are generally delegated to individual members. One individual in the group may be assigned the task of acquiring information for the group. On one hand, this may be considered an important lesson in the division of labor; on the other hand, it is a quick way of reducing the threshold of inconvenience of group work. The "research specialist," the one out of four or five in a group designated to conduct library research, is perhaps the only one who has developed realistic expectations for the search. Moreover, the time and effort spent researching for the group benefits the researcher but can lead to a gap in understanding what is available for the balance of the group members.

The observations clearly confirm students' predetermination of expectations. The relationship between user expectations and observed execution reveals a threshold in which expectations are optimized against trade-offs. The user's perceived utility of retrieval effort, cost, or time matches the optimal expectations, and they proceed to execute cost or time expenditures based on those expectations. Any expenditure beyond expectations is considered neither cost-effective nor optimal.

Thus, where reference librarians offer discussions of utility of resources as a critical point of entry into the reference process, this may result in modifying the users' perceptions of the research process, time expended, and value of effort expended. These discussions may center on clarifying the user's expectations regarding incremental expenditures of costs, time spent, pleasure or pain avoidance, and level of effort required to accomplish their goals. Theoretically, business librarians can pinpoint and adjust student perceptions through formal information literacy skills training by providing comparisons of the time and expenditures invested in retrieval of electronic resources versus print resources.

POST-REFERENCE PROCESS RESPONSE

The post-reference process response is defined as the user's reaction or response to retrieval in the reference process matching the predetermined expectations. As the observations indicate in this study, impatience results primarily from students' inability to meet expectations, and their perception that the research process is inconvenient. Even when the research process retrieves relevant and pertinent information within the need constraints, the reaction of satisfaction is minimized by demonstrations of impatience. This response spills over into future searches, so that impatience becomes incorporated into the pre-reference process stage of expectations.

Regarding group searches, the entire group will miss the opportunity of greater synergism if they do not share their findings in a matrix of communication. Often, as a result of this missed opportunity, many group members rely on each other for information, or on personal contacts as a primary source of information, placing trust in resources they have not personally reviewed. This observation is similar to findings in Auster and Choo's study identifying CEO preferences for personal contacts for information.

Students who search for themselves or as part of a group effort were observed as reacting to the reference process with a lack of patience, relative to other students in the library. Their time spent is perceived as non-tangible; if they do not see the end result immediately or if they are unable to access pertinent information in what they predetermine to be a timely manner, then the search may be viewed as a wasted effort. The reference librarian can work to change this reaction in the reference negotiation and in formal bibliographic instruction, encouraging the student to glean information even from a seemingly fruitless effort. There always is something to be learned from the search process, or even from a failure to retrieve the pertinent information.

If the student's expectations of an outcome do not match the actual retrieval, a form of dissonance may occur. Dissonance is defined as user recognition of the inability to achieve planned objectives. In an effort to alleviate this dissonance, include additional behaviors such as repeating the search, voicing frustration, or checking with the librarian. Some students may turn to fellow students or personal contacts rather than continuing the iterative process of the search, modifying, then redoing the search. Consequently, a range of response behaviors from satisfaction to dissatisfaction or dissonance provides the librarian with observable behavior cues, allowing identification of critical junctures in the reference process where the librarian can influence user thresholds of impatience and inconvenience.

CONCLUSIONS

In response to our initial question: Given recent rapid changes in information provision, computerized access, and the plethora of electronic resources, can we say user behavior has changed? The findings of this study and the literature indicate there are no absolutes for delineating behavior. However, we believe the evidence presented here justifies the assertions in the implications and conclusions. This study reveals observations that parallel findings of the past thirty years, pointing in the direction of continued user impatience and minimal student effort applied in the execution of search tasks. However, the recent enhancements in the availability of access to online services and electronic text have had an impact on user expectations. The perceived speed of electronic access has encouraged a greater dependence on electronic search tools than print tools. Faculty can have a strong impact in the query formulation stage of search behavior, primarily because of imposed assignments, though their recommendations of the use of both print and electronic systems can encourage a thorough research process. Information literacy programs and bibliographic instruction classes can modify unrealistic pre-reference process expectations and post-reference process responses by offering information seeking demonstrations that emphasize cost-effectiveness and time-efficiency when retrieving print resources versus electronic resources.

Future research may be conducted to develop a quantifiable model of information seeking. This may be accomplished by understanding the relationships of variables such as the predetermined quantity of information retrieved and quantity of time allocated in the library. These variables can be juxtaposed to develop a model of optimal cost-effective and time-efficient search behavior.

Additional research may involve analysis of the imposition of class assignments by business faculty, who by virtue of their suggestions for use of resources may transfer preferences for resources or time allocation. Furthermore, reference librarians should continue to examine the relationship between student expectations and the actual search outcomes, being sensitive to business students' propensity to apply attitudes of cost and time effectiveness.

REFERENCES

Auster, Ethel and Chun Wei Choo. "Environmental Scanning: A Conceptual Framework for Studying the Information Seeking Behavior of Executives." *Proceedings of the 54th ASIS Annual Meeting* in Washington, DC, October 27-31, 1991. Medford, NJ: Learned Information, 3-8, 1991.

Auster, Ethel and Chun Wei Choo. "Environmental Scanning: Preliminary Findings of Interviews with CEOs in Two Canadian Industries." *Proceedings of the ASIS Annual Meeting.* Medford NJ: Learned Information, 246, 1993.

Baker, Sharon, and F. W. Lancaster. *The Movement and Evaluation of Library Services,* 2nd ed. Arlington, VA: Information Resources Press, 1991.

Boyer, E. L. College: *The Undergraduate Experience in America.* New York: McGraw-Hill, 1987.

Gross, Melissa. "The Imposed Query." RQ 35(2):236-243, 1995.

Hawes, Douglass K. "Information Literacy and the Business Schools." *Journal of Education for Business.* September/October, 54-61, 1994.

Haythornthwaite, Jo. "Working with Business Information Today." *In The Business Information Maze: An Essential Guide.* London: Aslib, 1990.

Jones, Ann D., Richard Drapeau, and Lynn Godkin. "Library Utilization in Undergraduate Courses: Are Business Professors Using the Library?" *Journal of Education for Business.* December, 119-122, 1987.

Lavin, Michael. *Business Information.* Phoenix, Ariz.: Oryx Press, 1-14, 1987.

Lee, John W. and Raymond L. Read. "The Graduate Student and the Library." *College and Research Libraries* 33(5):403-407, 1972.

LittleJohn, Alice and Lois Benson-Talley. "Business Students and the Academic Library: A Second Look" *Journal of Business & Finance Librarianship* 1(1):65-74, 1990.

Mann, Thomas. *Library Research Models.* New York: Oxford University Press, 91-101, 1993.

Simon, Herbert A. "Rational Choice and the Structure of the Environment." *Psychological Review* 63, 2 (March), 129-38, 1956.

Smyth, A. Leslie. "Organization and Administration: Objectives, Planning and Staffing." In *Manual of Business Library Practice,* edited by Malcolm J. Campbell, 2nd edition. London: Clive Bingley, 23-39, 1985.

Zipf, George Kingsley. *Human Behavior and the Principle of Least Effort; an Introduction to Human Ecology.* Cambridge, Mass: Addison-Wesley Press, 1949.

The Reference Librarian
and the Business Professor:
A Strategic Alliance That Works

Paula J. Crawford
Thomas P. Barrett

SUMMARY. Strategic alliances are proliferating in the corporate world. They offer the participants an opportunity to pool limited resources, skills and capabilities to achieve common objectives that the partners may well be unable to achieve working alone. Strategic alliances can exist among a variety of partners, but making them work requires an understanding of common objectives, a commitment to those objectives and flexibility. The development of a successful strategic alliance between a university reference librarian and a business school professor is described. *[Article copies available for a fee from The Haworth Document Delivery Service: 1-800-342-9678. E-mail address: getinfo@haworth.com]*

Strategic alliances among corporations have proliferated in recent years as more and more firms have come to realize that carefully planned and executed collaborative efforts can enable them to accomplish together what they have neither the resources nor the capabilities to accomplish by working individually. Strategic alliances may take many forms, and may

---

Paula J. Crawford is Reference Librarian, and Thomas P. Barrett is Professor of Management (Retired), California State University, Stanislaus, Turlock, CA 95382.

[Haworth co-indexing entry note]: "The Reference Librarian and the Business Professor: A Strategic Alliance That Works." Crawford, Paula J., and Thomas P. Barrett. Co-published simultaneously in *The Reference Librarian* (The Haworth Press, Inc.) No. 58, 1997, pp. 75-85; and: *Business Reference Services and Sources: How End Users and Librarians Work Together* (ed: Katherine M. Shelfer) The Haworth Press, Inc., 1997, pp. 75-85. Single or multiple copies of this article are available for a fee from The Haworth Document Delivery Service [1-800-342-9678, 9:00 a.m. - 5:00 p.m. (EST). E-mail address: getinfo@ haworth.com].

75

operate under a variety of nameplates. However, the essence of all such alliances is that they are intended to be long-term cooperative undertakings that provide their participants with an opportunity to pool scarce or limited resources, skills, and capabilities to achieve common objectives.

Of course, strategic alliances do not have to be restricted to the corporate world. This article describes the development of a successful strategic alliance between a university reference librarian and a business school professor that evolved over a period of 15 to 20 years. The key players were Paula J. Crawford, the reference librarian, and Thomas P. Barrett, the business school professor. Crawford, although well-schooled in general reference, has no formal business background. Barrett is not a librarian. The impetus for their collaboration was threefold. First, they shared the belief that all business school students should possess the ability to find and use information in the library. Barrett recognized, in the mid-1970s, that many of the students in his senior level Business Policy course did not possess this ability and Barrett and Crawford were determined to remedy this, or at least, to alleviate some of its consequences.

BACKGROUND

California State University, Stanislaus is one of twenty-two campuses in the California State University system. It is a comprehensive four-year institution charged to serve the educational needs of persons in its six-county service area in California's San Joaquin Valley and Central Sierra foothills. Undergraduate majors are offered in more than 30 fields; graduate degrees are offered in six. While some on-campus housing is available, most students are commuters. Total enrollment is almost 6,000 students; full-time equivalent enrollment is approximately 4,500.

The University library is generally regarded by the faculty and students as the heart of the campus. Many faculty members consider the library to be the University's greatest strength. The library has approximately 310,000 volumes and is a partial depository for U.S. and California documents. The book and periodical collections have been developed to meet the needs of the curriculum. A full complement of library services, including reference, library instruction, computerized database searching and interlibrary loan, is available. The librarians have faculty status and are active in academic governance. The library supports the teaching mission of the University by encouraging critical thinking and lifelong learning through instruction in effective use and evaluation of information resources. Specifically, the library strives to ensure that all students leave the University with basic competency to find and evaluate information, with special emphasis on the major area of study.

The School of Business Administration enrolls about 20 percent of all students in the university. Degrees offered are: B.S. in Business Administration with concentrations in Accounting, Finance, General Business, Management, Marketing, and Operations Management; B.S. in Computer Information Systems; and the MBA. Both day and evening classes are offered on campus and evening classes are offered at the University's off-campus center in Stockton, 45 miles north of the university's Turlock campus. From the beginning, the faculty in Business Administration has aspired to professional accreditation by the American Assembly of Collegiate Schools of Business, and has structured its programs accordingly. However, resource limitations have precluded achievement of this goal to date. Currently, the School is a candidate for AACSB accreditation.

Undergraduate students in the School of Business Administration include traditional and nontraditional, day and evening, full-time and part-time, resident and commuter students. Primarily, they are first generation college students, transfers from local community colleges, commuters, and currently employed, either part-time or full-time.

The Business Policy course is the capstone course in the undergraduate Business Administration major. The course focuses on the chief executive officer of the business firm as the manager with responsibility for the totality of the enterprise in its environment, and on the CEO's role as the architect of organizational purpose and the builder of the organization. Following in the tradition of the Harvard Business School, this is primarily a case study course. The set of cases selected for a given class and the manner in which each case is to be approached is believed to be one of the most significant determinants of what the students learn in the course. Each case provides background materials facts, data, opinions, names, etc., dealing with an actual situation on a matter of significance, in a named firm—a situation that calls for management action. Students are charged to size up the situation facing the manager, and to formulate the most appropriate course of action for the manager to take in that situation. In each and every case study, heavy emphasis is placed upon helping the students develop skill in situational thinking, i.e., the ability to grasp, comprehend and deal with all the nuances, ramifications, and implications of each managerial decision situation. Through this, students are expected to deepen their knowledge and understanding of management and to further develop the skills and attitudes needed to effectively apply this knowledge.

PROBLEM RECOGNITION AND INITIAL RESPONSE

In the 1960s and early 1990s, Business Policy students were assigned cases at the rate of almost one case per week throughout the term. The cases were obtained from Harvard Business School, either directly or more often via text books, each containing a selected collection of cases. The cases themselves identified the issues of concern and provided salient background material. Students were expected to carefully scrutinize each assigned case to glean whatever insights into the situation might be contained therein. With sufficient experience, most students learned to do this reasonably well.

Beginning in the mid-1970s however, Barrett became increasingly dissatisfied with the results he was getting in class. He believed that the students' case analyses were often quite superficial and that they demonstrated a lack of awareness and/or understanding of significant, influencing trends and developments in the external environment of the firm. He gradually came to the conclusion that the root cause of this was that the cases themselves did not and could not provide the students with enough information to enable them to fully understand each decision situation. To obtain the needed information, additional research was believed to be absolutely essential.

Hypothesizing that a different approach built around intensive study of a smaller number of carefully selected cases would produce better results, Barrett changed the basic pedagogy of his course. The essence of the new approach was: (1) Barrett would select a set of four or five cases for the course; (2) each student would participate as a member of a three or four person team in the study of each case; (3) all case studies would entail a substantial research effort, i.e., including an environmental scan; and (4) all case studies would conclude with a written report prepared according to a prescribed format.

An environmental scan involves an effort to systematically explore the cultural, social, legal, political, demographic, economic, and competitive environments to identify likely major trends and developments that could impact the firm in the period ahead; and to forecast the probable behavior of each of these. An environmental scan is an essential precursor to sound planning because, if well done, it enables management to envision the key parameters of the environment within which the firm expects to operate in the period ahead.

Conducting an environmental scan is a challenging experience, however. It involves uncertainty, ambiguity, and stress because: (1) one cannot predict with certainty what the future will be like, and the signals that may provide clues to the future are often weak; (2) in conducting a scan, one can never be sure when the search is sufficiently thorough and when it is being needlessly drawn out; (3) it requires the exercise of a tremendous amount of judgment, and a willingness to take a stand to identify potentially significant trends and developments and forecast the probable behavior of each.

The new approach to cases had many consequences. The set of cases selected for study had to be restricted to those companies, industries, countries and/or regions, and time periods that were adequately represented in the library's holdings. Student researchers frequently uncovered inaccuracies and other shortcomings in published cases that had been assigned for study. The restrictions on case selections and the dissatisfaction with published cases eventually caused Barrett to discontinue all use of published cases around 1990. He developed his own cases from among firms that are known to be currently seeking to cope with selected strategic decision situations. Students began their research using the latest annual 10-K reports, proxy statements, etc., and went from there.

PANIC CITY

The students' responses to this new requirement quickly revealed that many of the students suffered from what Andrew Garvin calls "information paralysis"–that is, "the inability to proceed from a question to the actual act of beginning to gather the information needed for the answer" (Garvin, 1993). As Garvin explains, people with this condition "don't know what to do, when to start, or how to go about it. Fear takes over."

Students displayed their confusion and fear in a variety of ways. Some went to great lengths to seek a waiver of program requirements and exemption from the course; some simply dropped the course and put off a decision; some challenged the professor with claims such as: "I have a 3.0 GPA and I have never been to the library, so whey should I have to do this now?" Some helped to develop an active underground market for old case reports in the mistaken belief that these were the "holy grail"; and some went directly to the reference librarian with the request: "I'm studying Chrysler Corporation, tell me everything about the automotive industry."

It was at this time that Barrett approached Crawford and asked if she would be willing to provide his students with a brief introduction to the relevant business information sources in the library and to identify the types of information contained in each. From her position in Reference, Crawford had begun to appreciate the scope and magnitude of this problem. Crawford and Barrett both realized that by working together they could accomplish much more than they could by working individually. They decided to do so.

STRUCTURING THE ALLIANCE

The initial objectives of the new alliance were: (1) to provide students with a guide to selected reference sources of the university library (basic statistical sources, business and economic trends, industry statistics, company-specific information, etc.) tailored to the needs of students in the Business Policy course; and (2) to instruct students on how they might utilize these resources to find the information they would need for their case studies.

The centerpiece of this instructional effort was an in-class presentation by Crawford early in each term. This was accompanied by distribution of a handout Crawford prepared for the students to use throughout the term. The initial obligations that the alliance imposed on the new partners were relatively simple and straightforward, although there were some complications.

Barrett was to: (1) provide Crawford with an introduction to the case study pedagogy employed in the course; (2) adjust the course schedule to provide time for Crawford's presentation (and to schedule her presentation at the time when it would be most beneficial to the students and a time when they would be most receptive to this instruction); (3) to orient Crawford to the peculiarities of each assigned case and to the student requirements for each case study; and (4) select the cases to be assigned sufficiently in advance of the term so that Crawford could prepare.

Crawford was to: (1) identify any particularly significant gaps in the library's holdings that could and should be addressed; (2) to procure industry analyses, corporate reports and/or other documents that might be relevant; (3) select items that should be placed on reserve; (4) to determine ways to facilitate access to the resources and (5) prepare the handout and lecture notes.

Providing for the students at the off-campus center in Stockton required forethought and additional preparation for Crawford. University policy stipulated that classes in Stockton were to be the same in all respects as classes offered on campus. Since Stockton students (most of whom were part-time, evening students) could not be expected to journey 45 miles to campus to use the library, their university library arranged for them to use the library of San Joaquin Delta college, the local community college, and the Stockton-San Joaquin County Public Library. As might be expected, the resources of these libraries differed from those of the campus library. Therefore, Crawford had to familiarize herself with those collections, arrange interlibrary loans and prepare different handouts and lecture notes for use with the Stockton students.

Scheduling was also a sensitive matter for the library. Typically, Barrett taught two or three sections of Business Policy each term. Although some sections met twice a week for 1 ½ hours each time, and others met once a week for three hours, all sections were assigned the same set of cases, and all had the same set of requirements each week. The only difference among sections was the meeting time. When the course was scheduled in Stockton (usually once a year) Barrett commuted to Stockton and used the same cases and course requirements as on campus. This meant that sometimes as many as 75 to 90 students could be studying the same cases at the same time. Obviously, accessibility and efficiency were matters of continuing concern to all.

CHALLENGES

For her introduction to case study pedagogy, Barrett suggested Crawford read several works of Michael Porter. She also sat in on several business policy class sessions.

Timing library instruction was critical. While Barrett recognized the need for the instruction, he was hesitant to give up a lot of class time for it. The challenge was to give the students as much pertinent information in one session as possible without overwhelming them. Barrett scheduled it at the point when he grouped them into teams and the first case was assigned. This was important because the students were now eager and much more attentive. The students needed to be at a stage of desperation but not climbing the walls. Barrett always introduced Crawford to the class as the "best friend a Business Policy student could ever have." Recognition by the professor of Crawford's role helped the students to recognize the important part the library would play in their research.

Prior to each term Barrett met with Crawford to discuss the companies he had selected. He also outlined the "issues" of each case and provided the timetable for the reports. Then Crawford would proceed to research the companies to insure that students had enough relevant documents. Knowing the cases in advance allowed her to prepare some background information for each case. As students began to research their cases, the limitations of the library's holdings quickly became apparent.

Although the library had a good core business collection, what the students were seeking was industry specific, company specific and even geographically specific. The data had to be for a very specific time period as well. Because of the limited amount of time the student had for each case study (approximately two weeks per case) interlibrary loans did not provide much relief.

For several years Crawford wrestled with having to make what the library had work, while attempting to fill the gaps. The library responded to this challenge by expanding its paper collections of industry fact books and corporate annual reports, and by entering subscriptions to a carefully selected list of trade journals. This helped a little, but significant progress was not made until the library subscribed to a microfiche collection of annual and 10-K reports from Disclosure and microfiche versions of industry fact books found in the Statistical Reference Index collection. Later, the acquisition of Compact Disclosure on CD-ROM and Newsbank CD-ROM indexes and then access to Lexis/Nexis virtually eliminated this problem. The currency of the information available on Lexis/Nexis as well as its broad scope made more information available to the students than ever before. The Newsbank CD-ROM indexes helped to meet the need for geographically specific information. Many of the requirements of the environmental scan were met with microfiche collections of the Statistical Reference Index and the Index to International Statistics.

Crawford selected some items every term to be placed on reserve because the team approach posed a logistical problem for the library. Having three sections of the class working on the same case and needing access to the same information at the same time required solutions that were both efficient and practical. Crawford tried to anticipate which materials would be in high demand and put them on reserve. Students had to be cautioned that the fact that some document was "on reserve" did not mean it was "key" to the case, but simply a way to keep track of them.

Designing a handout for the students proved to be a challenge. While there was never any attempt to list every possible business tool, Crawford discovered the students were unfamiliar with the basic resources and had difficulty orienting themselves to the different areas of the library. The first handout was simply a list of those basic resources with their corresponding call numbers, such as business directories, periodical indexes, etc. This design was not effective because students were unable to connect the research tool with their need for information. Secondly, everything was not accessible in the reference area. The materials were spread out within the library and students had a difficult time locating them. The reference librarians decided a more convenient shelving arrangement might alleviate student frustration. Many of the major resources from the handout were brought together in one location. Then the design of the handout was re-worked to group the resources into sections to reflect the various aspects of the environmental scan. This design change allowed students the flexibility to start at the beginning of the handout and work straight through it or to divide the research among the team more easily. Having the handout in sections gave the students the flexibility to concentrate on the resources listed in any one section. The handout was entitled

"Search Strategy for Business Cases" to illustrate the procedure versus a bibliography.

In preparing her lecture notes, Crawford chose one of the cases to be studied as an example. Because the students did not intuitively understand how to use these tools, not only did the various tools need to be introduced, but a description of how to use them and an explanation of why students should use them became necessary. Using one of their cases to illustrate the use of the tools provided the hook Crawford needed to get and keep the students' attention.

Crawford's greatest challenge came with the introduction of the Lexis/ Nexis electronic database. When Lexis/Nexis was made available to the California State University system in 1992, Crawford saw the immediate advantage for Business Policy. Now, for the first time, students had access to more data and more current information than ever before. It also posed a dilemma: how to teach meaningful strategies for researching business cases online as well as continue to introduce the print resources in a single class session.

PROBLEMS

Barrett and Crawford worked together to resolve problems as they arose. Barrett found that the students were more interested in cases from emerging industries as opposed to the established ones which the textbooks offered. Using older cases presented additional problems for library research, too. Students needed to find information from prior years but it had to be information that would have been available at that time. Many of the sources students found gave historical data but that data would not have been available at the time of their case. Crawford had to not only assist them to find pertinent data but also to advise them to look at publication dates. Barrett's new approach to case selection effectively eliminated that problem.

Routinely at the end of each semester, the authors would compare notes regarding what went well and what did not, with each suggesting ideas for improvement. Crawford asked for clarification on those questions that had been problematic. Barrett polled his classes at the end of each semester and would pass on comments that might be worthy of consideration. It was at Barrett's suggestion that the handout was revised to include questions under each section relating to the environmental scan. It was Crawford who asked that the time allotted for library instruction be extended to allow more time for the online demonstrations.

There were some problems which one might expect from this type of collaboration. Students had a tendency to seek out the librarian who did the formal instruction, rather than ask questions of whomever was at the reference desk. Students had to be cautioned that Crawford would not write the report for them and students also had to realize that she had reference responsibilities to other students as well as to Business Policy students.

Using one of the actual cases as the example during the in-class presentation hooked the students early but also required making new handouts every term.

Some problems never went away. It was the nature of the class. The time frames within which each case study was to be completed were short. In an effort to imitate the real world, most cases were due within two to three weeks after being assigned. The team had to get together, decide on its approach to the case, divide the research up among the members, conduct the research, and write up the analysis in that period. Although the library acquired a number of new resources, no library can hope to fill every heavy workload required in the class. Barrett's reputation as a tough instructor was well known. Crawford found herself in the role of counselor and coach for the students. Upon the successful completion of the class some entrepreneurial students even sold T-shirts emblazoned with "Grin and Barrett" or "I survived Business Policy 19xx" to classmates.

OUTCOMES

Several positive outcomes resulted from this strategic alliance. The students became effective users of information. Over the years, former students have consistently heralded Business Policy with Barrett as the best experience they had; one in which they learned more than their other total academic experience combined. The skills they learned in that class prepared them so that they can now define their information needs. They learned to develop effective and efficient search strategies and they learned to be critical and to evaluate information. They became familiar with and consumers of periodicals they knew nothing about previously. They became more appreciative of the value of information. The librarian/professor collaboration in this class made the students active participants. They learned by doing and the authors learned that the timing of the library instruction portion was critical in that success.

WHERE DO WE GO FROM HERE?

The university reference librarian and business school professor strategic alliance is even more essential today. There is a shift in emphasis from

"Can we obtain information?" to "How do we evaluate all the information that is available?" Information resources are exploding on the Internet and more and more resources will be in electronic form. First, students will need to master the technology. Teaching students to think critically so that they can be selective and consider the reliability of the available resources will continue to be the roles of the reference librarian and the business professor. Students need to recognize the value of information and learn to make the cost for value tradeoffs. Continued collaborative efforts will be required if students are to be expected to be competent information consumers.

Barrett just recently retired but Crawford is hoping to maintain the alliance with his successor. The alliance may need to take on a different look but she is hopeful that she can maintain the cooperative spirit, personal commitment and equal partnership she and Barrett have shared. It has been said that "the hallmark of successful alliances that endure is their ability to evolve beyond initial expectations and objectives" (Bleeke, p. 127). The experience of Crawford and Barrett is proof of that statement.

REFERENCES

Bleeke, Joel & David Ernst. "The Way to Win in Cross-Border Alliances." *Harvard Business Review* Nov.-Dec. 1991: 127-135.

Garvin, Andrew P. *The Art of Being Well Informed. What You Need to Know to Gain the Winning Edge in Business*. Garden City Park, N.Y.: Avery Publishing Group, 1993.

Bibliographic Instruction
for Business Classes:
How to Avoid Information Overload

Barbara Huett
Amy Sims
Vanessa Villalon

SUMMARY. A contribution to an issue devoted to end-user re-search needs and information-seeking behavior, this paper describes a cooperative venture between faculty members, librarians and students to assess and improve methods of bibliographic instruction for business classes in order to assist students with their research needs.

At St. Edward's University's Scarborough-Phillips Library, bibliographic instruction (BI) of business information is offered to students upon the request of faculty members of the Business School–it is not a required credit course. A new approach to eliminating information overload in BI sessions was attempted, proved successful and will likely be repeated. *[Article copies available for a fee from The Haworth Document Delivery Service: 1-800-342-9678. E-mail address: getinfo@haworth.com]*

Barbara Huett is Library Director at Franklin College, Lugano, Switzerland. Amy Sims has worked for Dun & Bradstreet Information Services, Go Media, Inc. as Marketing Director, and most recently her own consulting business, Simsolutions, specializing in efficiency and technology consulting. Vanessa Villalon is a business management senior at St. Edward's University, and currently a teaching assistant for Professor Mark Poulos. She is presently interning at Doubletree Hotel, and plans to make her career in hotel administration.

[Haworth co-indexing entry note]: "Bibliographic Instruction for Business Classes: How to Avoid Information Overload." Huett, Barbara, Amy Sims, and Vanessa Villalon. Co-published simultaneously in *The Reference Librarian* (The Haworth Press, Inc.) No. 58, 1997, pp. 87-99; and: *Business Reference Services and Sources: How End Users and Librarians Work Together* (ed: Katherine M. Shelfer) The Haworth Press, Inc., 1997, pp. 87-99. Single or multiple copies of this article are available for a fee from The Haworth Document Delivery Service [1-800-342-9678, 9:00 a.m. - 5:00 p.m. (EST). E-mail address: getinfo@haworth.com].

Bibliographic instruction is offered in many forms, through the Scarborough-Phillips Library at St. Edward's University in Austin, Texas. The Scarborough-Phillips Library (SPL) is an academic library supporting the research needs of faculty, staff and students at St. Edward's University, a private, four-year, liberal arts college, which in addition to its undergraduate academic programs also offers two graduate degrees: Master of Business Administration (MBA) and Master of Arts in Human Services (MAHS).

This paper will focus solely on bibliographic instruction of business resources to undergraduate and graduate students, which in principle provides useful guidance for researching company and industry information to support coursework and research requirements. In designing a new approach to traditional BI delivery for such information, we believe that students may better learn methods for doing research. The advantages of gaining and retaining knowledge for research purposes will not only assist the student with current course requirements and assignments, but may also provide assistance later for job interviews, management issues in the workplace, decisions on making personal investments, etc.

At present bibliographic instruction (BI) to business classes is offered to students upon the request of faculty members at the Business School. It is not a required credit course; i.e., it is not a requirement for all business classes to receive BI. The faculty members who continually request BI sessions each semester teach both undergraduate and graduate courses in management, marketing and business policy. These sessions are scheduled according to coursework and time requirements. Additionally, many of the sessions are attended, in whole or in part, by the professor, who is thus able to observe the type of information the students receive.

As a result of past student evaluations of the BI sessions—as well as librarians' observations of business students' problems with information retention while working on their assignments and/or research after BI sessions—a different, and perhaps better approach to BI was recommended. However, despite professors' participation in BI sessions, very little feedback or evaluation was received from them concerning this problem. It must also be noted that other subject BI sessions were not necessarily modified based on these particular observations.

Nonetheless, one professor approached us with an idea to divide the BI sessions into two parts. He recommended that rather than combine demonstrations of both print and electronic resources in one session, the session would be split into two sessions, by scheduling the first only on print resources mid-way through the semester. Each session would ideally involve a 20-30 minute presentation. This approach might thereby reduce the "information overload" factor which appeared to contribute to many of the students' retention and comprehension problems, as well as general confusion with the materials presented. In addition, the completion of a library assignment would accompany this form of BI, and would be submitted to the professor by the end of the semester.

This recommendation originally proposed by Dr. Mark Poulos, a business faculty member, and assisted by our senior business librarian, Carla Felsted, was further developed by the principal author of this paper in order to improve the sessions' format and presentation. Also, in collaboration, two outstanding business students, one a recent MBA graduate, the other an undergraduate teaching assistant, present their evaluations and feedback on business BI.

ASSIGNMENT DESCRIPTION

The assignment [Figure 1] is based on a company name provided by the professor. Usually a list of companies' annual reports available at the Library is helpful to the professor to assign a company's name. Other times, the company's name is taken from textbook case studies. Each student is assigned a different company to research.

After the students complete the two BI sessions, the assignment sheet is handed out to them. They are generally given 2 weeks to complete the assignment; however, this varies according to professor and/or course. Evaluations at semester-end indicate that students are generally more successful at completing the assignment after attending the specialized BI sessions, rather than those who have not.

RESEARCHING BUSINESS INFORMATION: WHAT DO THEY NEED TO KNOW?

During the BI sessions, two handouts are given to the students–*Research Companies & Industries* [Figure 2] and *Business Research on the World Wide Web* [Figure 3]–the former given during the first session, the latter during the second session. After explanation and demonstration of the titles and sites listed on the handouts, the students are then able to pursue completing the assignment in the Reference Area. All reference librarians are informed of the assignment and prepared for the students' enquiries related to it.

The student researcher must decide which handout to use, and which

Principles of Management
Professor Mark Poulos

FIGURE 1

MANG-30
SUMMER 1996

COMPANY ASSIGNMENT _____

INSTRUCTIONS:

A. Investigate your assigned company using the resources of the Scarborough-Phillips Library, including both print and electronic sources. Consult the handout, *Researching Companies and Industries*, and request additional assistance from a Reference Librarian as needed.

B. Locate the information below, writing out the briefer answers, and photocopying the others. For each item, cite the source in which found.
    1. Company stock exchange symbol. (Consult "Stock Performance of Industries" section on handout)
    2. Mission Statement, philosophy or objectives for forthcoming year. (Consult Value Line, annual reports and/or current articles on the company)
    3. List of top officers. (Consult "Directories and Yearbooks" section on handout)
    4. College or university attended by the CEO or other top officer. (Consult Standard & Poor's Register or Who's Who in America)

    5. Standard Industrial Classification Code(s) and explanation. (Consult "Directories and Yearbooks" section on handout first, then Standard Industrial Classification Manual)

    6. Industry grouping in
        a) Standard & Poor's Industry survey
        b) Value Line

    7. Attach the page with ration information for the company's primary SIC Code from each of these:
        a) RMA Annual Statement Studies
        b) Almanac of Business and Industrial Financial Ratios
        c) Industry Norms and Key Business Ratios

    8. Name of ultimate parent or subsidiary companies, if any. (Consult "Directories and Yearbooks" section on handout)

    9. Most recent quarterly financial results. (Consult Value Line, S&P Cooperation Records, SEC's EDGAR on the Internet, and/or current articles)

    10. Company bond rating in
        a) Moody's
        b) Standard & Poors

    11. Current stock price (close on last business day).
        (Consult business/financial newspapers, or Internet sites)

    12. Company ranking (explain criteria for source selected from front of directory) (Consult Dun's Business Rankings or Ward's)

C. Locate three (3) articles about the company using INFOTRAC's Business Index ASAP, a full-text Internet database. Select topics related to text chapter headings. Attach the citations (including abstracts or in full-text form) to your assignment.

FIGURE 2. Researching Companies and Industries

Business Research on the World Wide Web
Selected Resources

ST.EDWARDS UNIVERSITY

General Business Sites:

Official Guide to Business School Web Pages. http://www.crimson.com
Updated irregularly, though consistently.

Texas Law Librarians. http://ccwf.cc.utexas.edu/~suefaw/
Provides links to a myriad array of legal resources for performing legal research, as well as links to administrative resources.

Business Law. gopher://fatty.law.cornell.edu
Originating at Cornell University, this is one of the best legal sources on the Internet. Includes Supreme court decisions, US, foreign and international law, as well as ADA legislation and the Uniform Commercial Code.

International Business Resources. http://ciber.bus.msu.edu/busres.htm
Michigan State University's Web site. Offers links to regional or specific country information.

Virtual International Business and Economic Sources.
http://library.uncc.edu/lis/library/using/services/reference
A metalink called VIBES to over 200 international business information sites.

Global Securities Information. http://www.gsionline.com

Financial and Economic Information. http://www.finweb.com
FINWeb at UT Austin lists resources on economic and finance-related topics. Geared mostly toward financial professionals.

Financial Reports. http://www.disclosure.com
Includes guides to understanding financial reports, as well as corporate financial reports and filing requirements, by subscription.

Stock Quotes. http://www.quote.com
Fifteen minute delay. Must register to use and fees required for some information.

Standard Industrial Classification. gopher://gopher.lib.virginia.edu
Free SIC code/industry listing.

Census Bureau Trade Information. http://www.census.gov

Cost of Living Index. http://www.homefair.com/homefair
This site has a national salary calculator which calculates cost of living in various cities.

Hoover's Online. http://www.hoovers.com
Directory of public and private companies. Profiles include company's email address.

Business Incubators. http://ra.cs.ohiou.edu
National Business Incubation Association's site devoted to the business incubation industry.

BizWomen. http://www.bizwomen.com
Online marketplace for business women. Includes useful resources, communications network, and other Internet links.

NYNEX Online Yellow Pages. http://www.niyyp.com
Free access to a directory of 16.5 million listings which aims to include virtually every U.S. business. Service is supported by advertising from interested businesses.

FIGURE 2 (continued)

Government Sites:

EDGAR. http://www/sec/edgarhp.htm
SEC's Electronic Data Gathering, Analysis and Retrieval System. Filings include public companies' registration statements, and periodic financial reports, such as 10-K annual reports, 10-Q quarterly reports, and 8-K current reports, as well as other documents.

GPO's Access to Federal News. http://www.access.gpo.gov
U.S. Government Printing Office's free access to same-day searching of *Federal Register, Congressional Record*, Congressional bills, and other government documents.

Library of Congress - LC WEB. http://www.loc.gov
Includes electronic exhibits, digitized projects, descriptions of collections, Library of Congress publications, and links to other LC systems, such as THOMAS full text database of congressional bills, and LC library catalog records. Also includes indexes to Internet resources.

National Trade Data Bank. htpp://www.stat-usa.gov
Commerce Department's comprehensive business and economic node on the Internet. More than 300,000 documents are available from over 20 federal sources, e.g. State Department, Treasury, Trade Commission, Federal Reserve, Small Business Administration, Social Security Administration, CIA, etc.

US Government Manual. http://compstat.wharton.upenn.edu:8001/~siler
Useful for understanding the responsibilities and structure of US government agencies. Includes telephone directory.

Federal Deposit Insurance Corporation (FDIC). gopher://sura.net

Newspapers and Newswires:

NewsPage. http://www.newspage.com
Updated daily, this site has over 600 sources covering 2000 topics.

Commerce Business Daily. http://www.govcon.com
Free access which includes search engine which allows reader to query the current issue or previous issues rather than scanning all the data.

Washington Post / Los Angeles Times. http://www.newsservice.com

San Francisco Chronicle/San Francisco Examiner. http://www.sfgate.com

PC Week Online. http://www.zdnet.com

Newswires. http://www.sage.hosting.ibm.com
A beta project from IBM, this service will deliver news reports to an email address or allow reader to read on WWW. Must download company-provided free software to indicate subjects of interest. Updated twice daily. Also has link to Reuters daily headlines.

NOTE: Use Yahoo search engine, and terms "states + newspapers" to explore other newspaper services on the Web. *Example*: http://search.yahoo.com/bin/search?p=states+newspapers

FIGURE 3. Business Information on the Web

Researching Companies & Industries

Standard Industrial Classification (S.I.C.) Codes

A number of sources list information about industries according to S.I.C. Codes; they are explained in: Standard Industrial Classification Manual. Ref / HF/ 1042/ S73/ 1987.

Industry Surveys

Inside U.S. Business: A Concise Encyclopedia of Leading Industries. Ref/ HC/ 106.8/ M337/ 1994.
Standard & Poor's Industry Surveys. Ref/ HC/ 106.8/ S74. Quarterly. 2 vols.
U.S. Global Trade Outlook. Ref/ HF/ 3031.U558. Starting 1995, continues U.S. Industrial Outlook.
U. S. Industrial Outlook. Ref/ HC/ 101/ U54. Annual (ceased 1994). Continued by U.S. Global Trade Outlook.
Value Line Investment Survey. Ref/ HG/ 4501/ V26. Consult Ratings and Reports volume, Industry Summary sheets. Also has pages for individual companies.

Directories And Yearbooks

These help determine how an individual company ranks within an industry, find parent and subsidiary companies, and locate specific company info. Browse Reference shelves for additional sources.

Directory of Corporate Affiliations. Ref/ HG/ 4057/ A219. 5 vols. Helps locate subsidiaries and parent company information for public, private and international firms.
Directory of Multinationals. Ref/ HD/ 2755.5/ S78. Has brief descriptions along with basic info.
Dun's Business Rankings. Ref/ HG/ 4057/ A237. Indicates how a company ranks within its industry.
Dun's Regional Business Directory. Ref/ HF/ 5068/ S3/ D7. 3 vols. San Antonio area includes Austin.
Fortune 500. A listing of the top 500 U. S. industrial companies, along with brief statistics, is published the last week in April/first week in May. Fortune Service 500 includes largest Commercial Banking, Diversified Financial, Retail and Transportation companies, and appears around the end of June.
Hoover's Guide to Computer Companies. Ref/ HD/ 9696/ C63/ US1835/ 1995.
Hoover's Guide to Private Companies. Ref/ HF/ 3010/ H6/ 1994-95.
Hoover's Handbook of American Business. Ref/ HG/ 4057/ A28617/ 1995. Profiles of 500 major U.S. companies.
Hoover's Handbook of Emerging Companies. Ref/ HG/ 4057/ A28618/ 1995.
Hoover's Handbook of World Business. Ref/ HG/ 4009/ H66/ 1996. Profiles of major European, Asian, Latin American, and Canadian companies.
Hoover's Masterlist of Major U.S. Companies. Ref/ HF/ 3010/ H67/ 1993.
International Directory of Company Histories. Ref/ HD/ 2721/ I63. Arranged by industries; indexed.
Moody's Industrial Manual and News Reports. Ref/ HG/ 4961/ M65. Hardbound and looseleaf volumes. See also the OTC Manual (Ref/ HG/ 4961/ M7237) for public companies traded over the counter.
Standard & Poor's Corporation Records. Ref/ HG/ 4501/ S76635. Loose-leaf set. Updated quarterly.
Standard & Poor's Register. Ref/ HG/ 4057/ A4. 3 vols:Corporations, Directors and Executives, Indexes.
Texas Business Directory. Ref/ HC/ 107/ T4/ T42. Compiled from Yellow Pages; useful for small businesses, professional firms, and non-profit organizations.
Texas 500. Ref/ HF/ 5065/ T4/ T49. Ranks Texas companies; largest ones are profiled; indexed by industry and location.
Ward's Business Directory of U. S. Private and Public Companies. 4 vols. Ref/ HG/ 4057/ A575/ 1995. Good for private companies; includes rankings within S.I.C. Codes.

FIGURE 3 (continued)

Financial And Operating Ratios

Dun & Bradstreet. Industry Norms and Key Business Ratios. Ref/HF/5681/R25/I525. Annual. Be sure to take note of fiscal year covered in this and below.
Robert Morris Associates. Annual Statement Studies. Ref/HF/5681/B2/R62. Annual.
Troy, Leo. Almanac of Business and Industrial Financial Ratios. Ref/HF/5681/R25/T68.

Stock Performance Of Industries

In addition to the below, consult Moody's Manuals and S & P Corporation Records. We also have a selected collection of annual financial reports shelved in Ref/HF/2.

Moody's Handbook of Common Stocks. Ref/HG/4905/M815. Also see Moody's Handbook of OTC Stocks for NASDAQ companies. Ref/HG/4501/M58.
The Outlook. Ref/HG/4501/S8353. In addition to a weekly article on the economic out-look and periodic economic projections, reviews specific stocks for investors. Weekly.
Standard & Poor's Stock Guide. Ref/HG/4915/S67. Monthly.
Value Line Investment Survey. Weekly Ratings and Reports. Ref/HG/4501/V26.

Bibliographies/Guides To Business Information

Daniells, Lorna M. Business Information Sources. Ref/HF/5351/D3/1993.
Encyclopedia of Associations. Ref/HT/17/G33. Lists many trade and industry organizations that you could write/call for information.
Irwin Business and Investment Almanac. Ref/HF/5003/D68a/1995.
Lavin, Michael. Business Information: How to Find It, How to Use It. Ref/HF/5356/L36/1992.
Popovich, Charles et. al. Directory of Business and Financial Information Services. Ref/HG/151.7/D57/1994.
Schlessinger, Bernard S. The Basic Business Library. Ref/HF/5351/B3/1995.
Woy, James. Encyclopedia of Business Information Sources. Ref/HF/5351/E5/1991-2.

Periodical Indexes And Other Electronic Sources

InfoTrac Business Index under the Scarborough-Phillips Library menu on the Campus-Wide Information System (CWIS). Articles with codes are on Business Collection microfilm.
InfoTrac Expanded Academic Index under the Scarborough-Phillips Library menu on the Campus-Wide Information System (CWIS). Some full-text articles.
Newspaper Abstracts on our library catalog includes the Wall Street Journal and New York Times.
Periodical Abstracts on our library catalog covers some business topics and has remote access.
Business Periodicals Index (Ref/Index Tables HF1/ B76) Paper subscription covers 1958-1990.
Austin American-Statesman (CD-ROM full text). Local business and company news.
FirstSearch - on SEU gopher (Ednet); articles indexing source; some full-text articles available. Individual search cards and instructions available at Reference Desk.
Edgar (SEC database) available on the CWIS (Campus Wide Information System) through Ednet, the SEU gopher, under the Into the Internet menu. Ask for assistance at the Reference Desk, or see the handouts in the Reference area to activate your computer account and for login instructions to access the CWIS.
Numerous DIALOG databases are searchable on request by Reference Librarians; we can also access the DataTimes on-line index to newspapers and newswires.

titles/sites on the handouts are essential for locating the company and industry questions on the assignment. His/her success of failure is based on identifying the relevant resource to the question at hand. Generally the assigned company is a public company for this assignment, thus alleviating difficulties in research strategies. Although, in some cases, the assigned company is a subsidiary, there are several "directories" sources listed on the *Researching Companies and Industries* handout which provide information for this type of company.

It was noticed by our librarians that prior to these BI sessions being divided into two presentations, the students appeared more confused as to what was expected of them, and made more errors in searching for the company and industry sources necessary to complete the assignment successfully. The assignment is found to be beneficial in saving classroom time, as well as one-on-one instruction by the reference staff, particularly for learning research basics for business information, as well as standard library reference materials.

STUDENTS' EVALUATION OF ASSIGNMENT

Amy Sims, MBA Graduate, May 1996

In today's "information age," one would think that business professionals would have a better handle on business reference and research. However, the fact is we are experiencing an "information research methods" overload. Back in high school and college, we all had our fair share of library sessions, book reports, term papers, research projects, and theses. But that happened when we were still standing in line for the card catalog. Microfiche was high-tech then! So for most MBA students, it has been a few years since we were required to tackle the library. Unfortunately, business research is not like riding a bike. If you have been away from it for any length of time, it is not easy to jump back into it. For many of the business professionals coming back to school, the multitude of on-line services, CD-ROM products, and proprietary information databases, not to mention the printed manuals and journals, can be completely overwhelming. New technology is changing so rapidly, enabling new and better methods of collecting and distributing data, that unless information and research happens to be your job, it is very difficult to keep up with it.

Walking into the Scarborough-Phillips Library at St. Edward's University can be a tumultuous experience for a business professional coming back to school after ten or so years. This is why a new approach to bibliographic instruction was so helpful. As MBA students, we needed to be able to find a lot of information, and we did not have a lot of free time to discover on our own how and where to find what we needed. Most MBA students have full-time jobs, and many have families as well. So, I was extremely grateful for the opportunity to experience in person the demonstrations of the various information sources available, both print and on-line.

Having worked for Dun & Bradstreet Information Services for nearly eight years, I was very familiar with the D&B publications, as well as business information in general. Yet, as I soon discovered, this had evolved into an unintended bias: I was unfamiliar with other, extremely useful reference sources, such as *Hoovers, RMA Annual Statement Studies,* and *Value Line.* These were sources that I later turned to for almost every case study I had in my Business Policy class that semester. What I discovered was that hands-on instruction had a much more lasting impression than if I had just been given a packet of information on the sources, and left on my own to find them. I was now able to visually place the directories and reports in the library, which enables faster and more efficient researching and information gathering on subsequent projects. The instruction was also helpful with the on-line session. A quick tutorial and visual walk-through of the log-in procedures for *InfoTrac's Business Index* allowed my own first attempt to run smoothly and without incident. I found that the most important benefit from the BI session was an increased awareness of the vast amount of information that is available, if only we know how to access it.

One important business distinction must be made regarding information research needs: it is not always—in fact not often—going to be historical. When we need information, it must be current. Last year's stock price is not going to be nearly as useful as today's. This is where on-line research comes in. The World Wide Web (WWW) is an incredible avenue for information research, but there are a few issues to consider. First of all, not all the information available is free, and if it is, it most likely will not be for long. The second issue is accuracy, and the ability to trust the source. Another issue is referencing the information. On my last project for business policy, my bibliography contained many URLs (Uniform Resource Locators), or WWW addresses, as references, and many of the articles were also obtained via the WWW. These sources are constantly changing and moving, and it is extremely helpful to have a list of these sources available at the library when time is a limited resource.

My BI session happened to be in one evening, and I found this approach to be very helpful. Because of the nature of my courses, I needed to be able to do research immediately, and waiting several weeks for the second half would have been detrimental to my case studies. The two-session approach would really only be beneficial to MBA students if the sessions were given in consecutive class periods. This way, the students would not feel overwhelmed by receiving all of the information, both print and electronic, in one session, but they would still receive the information early on in the semester and be able to use it immediately.

The usefulness of the BI sessions provided at the Scarborough-Phillips library does not end with school. In today's business climate, information is the key to success, and it is just as important to be able to research for a job as it is for a school project. An MBA may get you a job, but the ability to find and discern current business information will help you keep it.

Vanessa Villalon, Undergraduate Business Student

My experience after the library exercise led to successful presentations in two business courses: Business Policy and Small Business Management. The Business Policy class required a group research paper and an analysis of an existing business. The assigned company was Nestle. The Small Business Management class required writing a formal, comprehensive feasibility and analytical study of a proposed small business venture. The BI exercise showed me new ways to find materials needed for my research papers.

Based on the first BI session, the preliminary step I took was to open my student computer account in order to access information from the *InfoTrac's Business Index*. Instructions on how to activate and access the computer account were presented in the BI session. Afterwards, I used the handouts accompanying the library assignment as a guide to find the materials I needed. These handouts listed resources in which I could find information on the company assigned. I was able to identify these resources because the librarian displayed and passed the books around during the BI session, so that the students could become familiar with them. The second BI session covered available electronic resources relevant to the assignment.

The Business Policy coursework required the group to identify the corporation, where it is based, and where its major operations are conducted. In addition, we had to identify major product lines, major markets, customers served, as well as track sales activity, analyze the activities of the firm, determine major competitive threats and competitive opportunities, and finally recommend future strategies. The Small Business Management course required us to submit an abstract, a transmittal letter, an identification of the industry and organization, business operation information, a market review, financial analysis, and conclusion of the business venture.

Both assignments required using resources in the library, especially periodical literature. The research paper for the Business Policy class had to contain statements of the CEO in the Annual Report to Stockholders; any other public statements by the CEO in the business press, statements contained in the Annual 10K Report to the SEC, an analysis of the corporation in *Value Line,* or by any other investment advisory service. The annual report for Nestle was very thorough, and achieved its purpose for completing the research paper. Some of the resources used for the small business venture were *Census '90, State Rankings 1996, Demographics USA,* and the *Gale Book of Averages.*

After the library BI sessions, the library staff was very cooperative whenever the group had a question or concern about the materials needed for the research project. I received help especially on the small business venture which required a lot of research. The BI sessions helped me become familiar with the organization of the library and the resources available to help me succeed in my assignments for coursework. I regret not having the chance to receive bibliographic instruction as a freshman or sophomore at St. Edward's. I believe all business students should be familiar with library resources due to the requirements and demands of professors to become successful students in their classes. It is also essential that the World Wide Web be introduced to students for business research. This attracts students' attention, and shows them the convenience of retrieving information at their fingertips. I would also recommend that this type of library exercise become mandatory for all students.

In conclusion, the business BI sessions and accompanying assignment are great introductory tools to business research. Dividing the sessions into two parts enabled me to understand the information so I could use it effectively in my classes. The first session introduced print resources to the class. I observed that the class had no interest in the presentation given by the librarian. However, I found the information beneficial to my future assignments. The second session introduced electronic resources. This session was interesting and kept the class focused on the librarian's presentation. I believe the BI sessions should be scheduled having the electronic resources session held before the one which presents the print resources. The BI sessions should entice the students to learn the information, and I feel this order would meet those needs.

CONCLUSION

Although evaluations vary in opinion and suggestion concerning the design, format, and scheduling, this type of business BI is essentially provided to increase the student's knowledge of sources available, to guide them through the assignment, and to enable them to utilize what they have learned for future assignments and research requiring the library's resources.

AUTHOR NOTE

Barbara Huett received her MLIS from University of Texas at Austin in 1991, and co-authored *The Basic Business Library: Core Resources*, 3rd ed., Bernard Schlessinger (ed.). Amy Sims is a May 1996 MBA graduate from St. Edward's University.

REFERENCES

Baker, Sharon L. and F. Wilfrid Lancaster. *The Measurement and Evaluation of Library Services*, 2nd Edition. Arlington, Virginia: Information Resources Press, 1991. 205-206.

Kaiser, Paula R. and Catherine K. Levinson. Teaching Company Research: Step-by-Step Instructions for Guiding Students Through A Library Assignment. *Bulletin of the Association for Business Communication?* Sept. 1994 v57 n3, 12(5).

Richardson, Steve and Lew Stratton. Providing the "Best Possible Access." *Online*. Jan 1994 66-70.

CREDITS

Carla Martindell Felsted, Senior Business Reference Librarian, Scarborough-Phillips Library, St. Edward's University, Austin, Texas.

Mark Poulos, Ph.D., Professor, School of Business Administration, St. Edward's University, Austin, Texas.

Reference Services
and Collection Development
Faculty Outreach
Through the Campus Network

Elizabeth A. Simmons
Randall M. Macdonald

SUMMARY. Effective reference services and collection development in a small academic library depend upon collaborative planning and performance by the entire library staff. Coordination of library activities and understanding of the library and college
mission are the foundations of a program responsive to the needs of
the college community. Partnerships between the library and classroom faculty ensure that curricular needs are satisfied through activities as diverse as bibliographic instruction and materials acquisition. Traditional interactions have been greatly enhanced through
rapid advances in telecommunications, offering librarians additional
tools for faculty outreach. *[Article copies available for a fee from The
Haworth Document Delivery Service: 1-800-342-9678. E-mail address:
getinfo@haworth.com]*

Elizabeth A. Simmons is Reference Librarian, and Randall M. Macdonald is
Collection Development Librarian, Florida Southern College, 111 Lake Holling-
sworth Dr., Lakeland, FL 33801-5698.
The authors wish to thank Ellen Cannon for her assistance in preparation of
this manuscript.

[Haworth co-indexing entry note]: "Reference Services and Collection Development Faculty Outreach Through the Campus Network." Simmons, Elizabeth A., and Randall M. Macdonald. Co-published simultaneously in *The Reference Librarian* (The Haworth Press, Inc.) No. 58, 1997, pp. 101-106;
and: *Business Reference Services and Sources: How End Users and Librarians Work Together* (ed:
Katherine M. Shelfer) The Haworth Press, Inc., 1997, pp. 101-106. Single or multiple copies of this article
are available for a fee from The Haworth Document Delivery Service [1-800-342-9678, 9:00 a.m. - 5:00 p.m.
(EST). E-mail address: getinfo@haworth.com].

101

BACKGROUND

Roux Library serves a population of 1,625 full-time undergraduate students at Florida Southern College in Lakeland, a four-year institution with a strong liberal arts tradition. A single master's degree program is offered in business administration with an enrollment of sixty students. Undergraduate programs with the largest student enrollments include business, education, and natural sciences. The library's general collection includes over 130,000 book volumes and seven hundred fifty periodical subscriptions, and a burgeoning multimedia collection numbering several hundred items.

Historically the library has enjoyed strong support from the administration and faculty. An important component of this relationship has been active participation in the development of the collections on the part of numerous faculty members. Through the summer of 1996 library acquisitions were handled by the same librarian for several decades, and the precise nature of materials selection was managed effectively by this person. She had an uncommon cross-disciplinary familiarity with the school's programs and collections, and enjoyed a good rapport with the faculty.

A NEW FOCUS

The last several years have witnessed a renewal for the college in enrollment—up over fifteen percent since 1994-1995—and in capital expenditures for technologies. The Fall 1996 semester brought a campus-wide information network to the college for the first time, supplemented by full graphical Internet access. Concurrent with these evolving campus services has been a re-emphasis and improved funding from top administrators to enhance the library's book collections, especially in business and economics to support the MBA program.

Establishment of the library's place on campus in the rapidly changing atmosphere of the administration's new focus for library development and the advent of the campus network became a central focus for our library and its staff. Reference and collection development librarians have worked to develop several processes which improve interaction with the faculty and increase library visibility on campus.

Faced with the prospect of new technologies, decisions had to be made regarding how we could best utilize network resources to enhance the services and image of the library. Drawing upon our own experience with the Internet and the World Wide Web—which averages four years among the several principal librarians involved—the group established a series of goals which slowly eased faculty inexperienced with online resources into library involvement.

PROGRAM GOALS

Taking advantage of the opportunities a campus network affords a small college community became a vital element in the library's pursuit of its mission. The library has actively incorporated the improved campus telecommunications into its public and technical services programs, and has seen enhanced interactions with the campus community. This has been accomplished through three distinct goals, each utilizing campus network resources:

1. To demonstrate leadership on campus by displaying the tangible benefits of network communication.
2. To further solicit faculty involvement in campus library services, especially important as we undergo reaccreditation studies during the next two years.
3. To coordinate interdepartmental library outreach activities.

Leadership

Establishing the Library as the Pacesetter of Campus Network Use

As many smaller colleges make the transition to campus networks and Internet access, the role of the library must change to encourage and embrace the available technologies. Librarians have traditionally been among the first on campus to gain practical experience with new technologies–audio-visual equipment, automated systems, and the Internet included. This exposure places a certain amount of responsibility on the library staff–faculty and students now regularly consult the librarians for assistance in using Internet and network resources.

Interactions such as these have provided additional opportunities for technology-supported library instruction. These have taken the form of evening workshops dedicated to locating online resources for research and introducing strategies for evaluating the quality of material retrieved. Preparation for these sessions included purchase of a thirty-five inch monitor, linked to a network-connected personal computer through a PC-to-TV converter. Open to faculty and students, these well-attended sessions have served as a relaxed first look for new network users at the wealth of material now accessible to our campus.

General library information is available through the Roux Library home page, which was established during the summer of 1995 (*http://snoopy. tblc.lib.fl.us/fsc/roux.html*). This page is publicized during registration and throughout the year in an effort to provide the most current information about library programs and services. Availability of the campus network and Internet services has corresponded with an increased number of hits to the page, which while difficult to qualify may indicate a heightened awareness of the library.

Our page has served as a local model for academic department home page development, and we have provided HTML and design assistance across campus. A combination of original content and links to remote sites demonstrates the essential utility of a page as an information source and public relations tool, and serves as one component of our outreach to faculty. Present plans include development of an online library newsletter, comprehensive lists of titles recently acquired, and online book request forms for Interlibrary Loan and materials acquisitions.

Faculty Outreach

Promoting Faculty Involvement in Library Services

The Florida Southern College Library has relied heavily upon faculty involvement to assist in developing and maintaining collections matching curricular needs. Established liaison assignments are handled by library staff in an effort to maintain consistent contact with departments. Librarians are assigned departments, divisions, or subject areas consistent with their expertise, and maintain an awareness of areas for library improvement. The use of new techniques and telecommunications is built upon this proven method of cooperation and dialogue between the library and faculty—new methods of outreach do not stand alone or replace but supplement and broaden the existing systems.

Campus networks provide many opportunities for faculty outreach beyond individual contact and departmental liaison duties. Librarians can use enhanced communication technologies to reach a broader range of the campus community. Electronic communication in the form of e-mail and Internet access have allowed us at Florida Southern College to improve our methods of outreach and cooperation with faculty.

Campus e-mail capabilities, including distribution lists, allow librarians to disseminate information regarding availability of new acquisitions and library programs to individuals and groups of faculty. Faculty members are notified of purchases made at their request and of materials matching faculty-supplied lists of personal and professional interests. Information sharing is not limited to news of print resources—librarians working from current awareness lists or from personal knowledge of faculty interests send URLs of applicable Web sites for faculty review or incorporation into class assignments. Reliance on the campus mail delivery system has diminished, and faculty response to the immediacy of our services has been positive.

Mailing lists allow for the rapid and reliable distribution of information to groups of faculty members with common interests. Beyond the expected groups consisting of all instructors in a given department, the mailing lists include subsets of departments and groups that cross departmental lines. For example, those faculty members teaching courses to MBA-program students compose a subset of the business department mailing list and selected additional faculty from the social sciences division.

An undergraduate cross-disciplinary women's studies course is taught each semester at Florida Southern College. Faculty members from departments as diverse as economics, art, history, English, and mass communications are represented in this group. A mailing list of all faculty members participating in the course is maintained. Information regarding the acquisition of materials related to women's studies is distributed to all of these individuals via one mailing list. Mailing lists allow the library staff to maintain records of interest profiles in a format that also eases the distribution of the information.

Interdepartmental Coordination

Library Departments Working Together for Outreach

The chemistry among small library staffs affects the number and quality of services provided. Interdepartmental cooperation is a necessary, useful part of presenting the library as a unified, efficient, and integral department on campus. Close working relationships between public services and technical services eliminates duplication of effort, makes the information provided to faculty more comprehensive and presents information in a usable, compact format. The library is presented as one body working together to support the teaching faculty.

What began as a unique program goal has subsequently enabled other goals to be achieved more readily, and has provided benefits to librarians individually. An improved appreciation for the relationships between various library functions has resulted, permitting a more coherent approach to planning and delivery of library services. This appreciation has also fostered collegial, mutually supportive staff relationships where professional successes of the group and group members are celebrated.

PRELIMINARY FINDINGS

Following a semester of application, enthusiasm among the librarians for network-supported communications and faculty outreach has increased. There is not yet enough quantifiable data to draw specific conclusions about the effectiveness of our efforts beyond the relative impressions we have formed. The online training sessions are unlike any services previously offered–students and faculty have shown through their attendance an interest in library and network services, and learn first-hand what the librarians have to offer professionally. An early estimate indicates that faculty participation in acquisitions has increased nearly two-fold compared to the 1995-1996 academic year.

We now have the potential to reach "virtually" every person on campus–everyone who checks e-mail receives regular communication from the library. Positive patron feedback has encouraged us to develop additional technology-supported projects, and we look forward to building on the strong foundation we have established.

Index

ABI/Inform, 10
  business students' familiarity
    with, 64
ACCESS, 7
Accounting information, for school
    business officials, 18
Alta Vista (search engine), 33-34
American Assembly of Collegiate
    Schools of Business, 6,8,77
American Express, 31
American Graduate School of
    International Management
    (Thunderbird)
  alumni network, 7
  English as Second Language
    students' corporate research
    project, 2,5-12
  classroom setting for, 6-8
  course-specific website
    development for, 8-10
  effectiveness of website, 10
Annual reports, on World Wide Web
    corporate home pages, 31
Apple, 36-37
Association of School Business
    Officials, Internet website
    for, 13-26
  information and services available
    on
  accounting resources, 18
  bank-related information and
    services, 18,22
  benefits to librarians of, 23-24
  benefits to primary user
    populations of, 24-25
  commercial websites, 18,20
  credit card services, 18,22
  external user's role in
    development of,
    15-17,24-26

funds transfer services, 22
government business
    resources, 20
html script development for, 24
investment resources, 20-21
legal and legislative resources,
    21
newspapers, 21
publication services, 21
"A School Business Officials'
    Pathfinder" for, 17-18,19,23
security for, 21-22
tax information, 22
technology software and
    hardware information,
    22-23
website availability, 23
website design, 17-23
AT&T, 28,50-51
Audi, 30
Automated Clearinghouse, 22

Babson College, 20
Bank-related data and services, 18,22
Barrett, Thomas P., 76,78-81,83-85
Belk College of Business
    Administration, 8
Bell South, 16
Ben & Jerry, 29
Bibliographic instruction, in business
    resources, 87-99
  "information overload" in, 88-89
  print resource instruction
    component of, 88-89
  research assignment in
    handouts for, 89-95
  students' evaluation of, 95-99
BigBook (corporate home page
    directory), 37-38

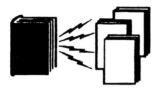

Haworth
DOCUMENT DELIVERY
SERVICE

This valuable service provides a single-article order form for any article from a Haworth journal.

- *Time Saving:* No running around from library to library to find a specific article.
- *Cost Effective:* All costs are kept down to a minimum.
- *Fast Delivery:* Choose from several options, including same-day FAX.
- *No Copyright Hassles:* You will be supplied by the original publisher.
- *Easy Payment:* Choose from several easy payment methods.

Open Accounts Welcome for . . .
- Library Interlibrary Loan Departments
- Library Network/Consortia Wishing to Provide Single-Article Services
- Indexing/Abstracting Services with Single Article Provision Services
- Document Provision Brokers and Freelance Information Service Providers

MAIL or *FAX* THIS ENTIRE ORDER FORM TO:

Haworth Document Delivery Service
The Haworth Press, Inc.
10 Alice Street
Binghamton, NY 13904-1580

or FAX: 1-800-895-0582
or CALL: 1-800-342-9678
9am-5pm EST

PLEASE SEND ME PHOTOCOPIES OF THE FOLLOWING SINGLE ARTICLES:
1) Journal Title: _____
    Vol/Issue/Year: _____ Starting & Ending Pages: _____
Article Title: _____

2) Journal Title: _____
    Vol/Issue/Year: _____ Starting & Ending Pages: _____
Article Title: _____

3) Journal Title: _____
    Vol/Issue/Year: _____ Starting & Ending Pages: _____
Article Title: _____

4) Journal Title: _____
    Vol/Issue/Year: _____ Starting & Ending Pages: _____
Article Title: _____

(See other side for Costs and Payment Information)

COSTS: Please figure your cost to order quality copies of an article.

1. Set-up charge per article: $8.00
   ($8.00 × number of separate articles) _____

2. Photocopying charge for each article:
   1-10 pages: $1.00 _____

   11-19 pages: $3.00 _____

   20-29 pages: $5.00 _____

   30+ pages: $2.00/10 pages _____

3. Flexicover (optional): $2.00/article _____

4. Postage & Handling: US: $1.00 for the first article/
   $.50 each additional article _____

   Federal Express: $25.00 _____

   Outside US: $2.00 for first article/
   $.50 each additional article_____

5. Same-day FAX service: $.35 per page _____

GRAND TOTAL: _____

METHOD OF PAYMENT: (please check one)

❑ Check enclosed ❑ Please ship and bill. PO # _____
(sorry we can ship and bill to bookstores only! All others must pre-pay)

❑ Charge to my credit card: ❑ Visa; ❑ MasterCard; ❑ Discover;
❑ American Express;

Account Number:_____ Expiration date:_____

Signature: **X**_____

Name: _____ Institution: _____

Address: _____

_____

City: _____ State:_____ Zip:_____

Phone Number: _____ FAX Number: _____

MAIL or *FAX* THIS ENTIRE ORDER FORM TO:

Haworth Document Delivery Service
The Haworth Press, Inc.
10 Alice Street
Binghamton, NY 13904-1580

or FAX: 1-800-895-0582
or CALL: 1-800-342-9678
9am-5pm EST)